IF YOU'VE BEEN THINKING THAT
GOING TO CHURCH ON SUNDAY
AND BIBLE STUDY ON WEDNESDAY
IS ALL THERE IS

You may want to sit down for this

*"If God waited on people to become perfect
before He anointed them
to preach, teach, lead or minister,
there would never be anyone worthy,
and the work would never get done.*

*God uses willing vessels, with weaknesses,
so His strength, power, and anointing,
can shine through,
and He can get the glory!"*

Keith Hammond

Church On Sunday
Nothing On Monday

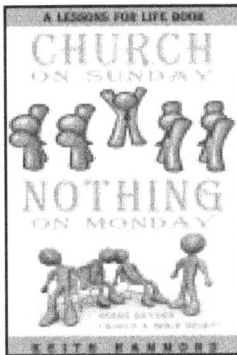

Going Beyond
Church and
Bible Study

Cover Art Purchased and Used With Permission From Leo Blanchett
Cover Layout and Interior Design: Keith Hammond

Lessons For Life Books

PUBLISHERS

L E S S O N S F O R L I F E B O O K S . C O M

LessonsForLifeBooks.com

IMPRINT A Lessons For Life Book

Church On Sunday
Nothing On Monday

*Going Beyond Church
and Bible Study*

© 2012 by
Keith Hammond
is published by
Lessons for Life Books, Inc.
7455 France Ave. S. #305
Edina, MN 55435

Inquiries should be addressed in writing to:
Lessons For Life Books
7455 France Avenue South #305
Edina, MN 55435
or by email to:
permissionrequest@LessonsForLifeBooks.com

ISBN-13: 978-1-938588-12-9
Library of Congress Control Number: 2012915234
Printed in the U.S.A.

Dedication

God Almighty,
I give you all the glory, honor, and praise for all that you have done
and still do in, to, and through, my life.
Thank you for Jesus Christ and the Holy Spirit,
and for the redeeming power of your Love.

To my wife,
in this 28th year together,
thank you for all your prayers and patience.

To my daughters,
my Love for you goes beyond words.
Many blessings to you both.

To my grandsons,
it is a great joy
to be Blessed with your presence in our lives.

To the Hammond and Fitzpatrick families,
I pray that you will unite arm in arm one day
and allow yourselves to be encircled by
the healing power of God's Love.

To Pastor Arthur Agnew,
only God could know how grateful I am,
for the 10 years you stood by my side.
Your training and teaching and telling will always be with me.

Acknowledgement

Ken E. at MMS,
I thank God for using you to be the springboard
that helped launch this ministry.
Thank you for the open door.
I'm forever grateful.

Dana Lynn Smith
The Savvy Book Marketer
Your wisdom, knowledge & understanding,
are incredible and inspiring.
Thank you for being my coach.

There are others who at some point and time of my life,
made a measurable impact, whether good or bad,
I am thankful for your input into me,
as it helped God prune, grow and mature me in more ways,
than you will ever know.

God Bless You All.

Introduction

On Sunday morning in many churches all over the world, members flock into the four walls of the Sanctuary, settle in their seats, and open their eyes to be entertained, and their ears to hear a sermon. Many of the people in the seats and pews are only there for those reasons. To hear songs, get the sermon, and leave. This is what pastors mean when they prompt you not to leave the same way you came.

God's Word is designed to *feed you, empower you,* and *light a fire within you* so that what you hear from the preacher *prompts you* into being passionate about the message to the point of wanting to DO what it says. The Bible says be ye doers of the word and not hearers only. It seems, that we have raised a generation of hearers, who need to keep hearing the message over and over again, just to stay fed, rather than getting full and putting that faith into action.

But how can you change this weekly ritual? How can you as a church member stop limiting yourself to song and sermon, embrace the Ministry of Jesus, and come alive with the passion that Jesus walked in daily? It's quite simple, and I'm going to teach you how.

The responsibility of every Christian is to learn the difference between church and ministry, and why we can't have one without the other, we must do both. Most Christians are used to just having church on Sunday, then doing nothing on Monday or the rest of the week, except Bible study on Wednesday nights. This man-made tradition has stood as the glass ceiling over the growth of many Christians for many decades. Our focus must be to break through that barrier.

Church On Sunday Nothing On Monday is a Ministry Curriculum. Some church leaders have walked away from ministry and mission, to embrace membership and money. This digression has transformed some churches into mega-centers full of people with faith but no works. The ministry of Jesus is in direct opposition to faith without works. Based on Matthew 25:35-36 and James 2:14-26, this book can help light your fire, ignite your passion, and help you get out of tradition and routine!

There are churches that exist just to have church. Ministry work is nonexistent. God's Word is placed on the heart of the preacher who is supposed to preach it. But IF the preacher who receives the message from God, does not pass it on to you, then all you're getting is a personal interpretation of the message, which will do nothing more than make you leave hungrier than you came, because you haven't been fed that day. And, you keep coming back week after week looking to be fed, rather than learning how to take what you've eaten, move beyond the message, grow up, so you can learn how to feed others.

Getting fed by a preacher these days is easier than you think. There are thousands of sermons available on the Internet. I'm one who admits that as a man of God, when I'm spiritually hungry I use this magnificent technology tool for one of the good purposes intended, and eat of the word, through the preacher delivering it. But please hear this next statement, because it is vital to your growth. If you are a person who does not have a church home because you feel that you can get the word at home through the Internet or on television, you are missing the most valuable part of the message: the assembling, gathering, fellowship, and relationship with God's people. Let me explain, using three scriptures.

1. Genesis 2:18

God Himself said it is not good for man to be alone. So God created another person for man to have a relationship with & get help from.

2. Mark 6:7

After Jesus had trained His disciples He called them to Himself and then sent them out two by two. There are many reasons for using two people to carry out the assignment including safety, accountability, and because when two or more are gathered in His name, and in His will, they are given whatever they ask.

3. Hebrews 10:25

The assembling of ourselves together with other saints helps us remember that we are not alone in our walk, or our ministry. This is why just watching a sermon on TV at home is NOT ENOUGH.

Jesus never intended for Christians to get comfortable with just coming to church on Sunday and Bible Study on Wednesday, with no ministry work during the week. THIS IS NOT WHAT BEING A CHRISTIAN IS ABOUT. There is much more to it.

Many Christians have become comfortable sitting in the pews of churches on Sunday waiting to hear the latest spin on, and title of, the sermon. This truly has become a ridiculous tradition. I've mentioned in many of the books I've written, that the members who have settled into this routine, are only partly responsible for their actions. The other responsible party is the leader themselves. Why? Because sheep can't lead sheep. And if the sheep are sitting in the pews waiting for direction, assignment, anointing, or to be told, shown, trained on what to do next, but the leader either doesn't know or is afraid to tell them because of personal fears that they may walk into their calling and not come back, it is a travesty on both sides.

The Ministry of Jesus was and is still quite simple.
- Feed the Hungry
- Clothe the Naked
- Visit the Sick
- Minister to Prisoners
- Help Strangers
- Take care of Widows and Orphans

It takes compassion to do ministry work. And Jesus led the way by teaching, training, and showing us how to do these things and more.

But we've gotten so far away from these basic standards, that social service agencies had to be formed to do what Christians would not.

Typical in most churches today is the routine to go eat after church on Sunday. That's either at home around the table, or out to a restaurant. This routine has gotten so bad in some churches that it has become a form of gluttony, and a ritual, rather than anything resembling a social gathering and fellowship of the saints.

When members fall into this routine (including the pastor, priest, and bishop), they take the power of the anointed sermon that was just preached, and lessen it. Why? Because if you were just fed spiritually by a powerful message, natural food would be the last thing on your mind. You would be so full of the spirit of God's word being preached into your hearing, that you would be empowered to want to go and DO something with it. Instead, most Christians have no clue what to do next, and settle for going out to eat, slipping right back to the same routine of doing nothing during the week, and returning to church next Sunday to do it all over again.

What good is it to be on fire on Sunday, do no ministry work at all during the week, only to return to hear another good sermon next week? Tell me if I'm wrong, but does this sound like anything JESUS would do? Absolutely NOT! Jesus would preach a great sermon, then take His flock out to serve by feeding people, clothing them, visiting and healing the sick, ministering to prisoners, helping strangers, and other powerful ways to draw people to Himself. Jesus would never settle for just sitting down and rubbing an overly full belly after having the fire inside Him ignited by a great sermon.

Someone needs to tell you and others that after church on Sunday, you should be so fired up from the sermon that you 'want' to go out and DO something with that fire. That is the very reason I believe God prompted and inspired me to write this book. To deliver a reminder to Christians all over the world that may have settled into the routine and ritual of just attending church on Sunday, Bible Study on Wednesday, and doing nothing at all for God during the week.

In another book of mine titled, *"Transform Your Schedule Transform Your Life"* I've placed numerous activities that you can choose from to do ministry work during the week, starting with just one hour. But, as I'll explain in detail why it takes a sacrifice of time to make this happen, I'll also help you to understand just how to do that.

God wants people who are willing to set aside their own schedules for the purpose of helping to win souls for the Kingdom of God. Your schedule, more than likely, has no eternal purpose. But God's schedule, is all about eternity. And you, can be one of His chosen vessels, hand picked and selected for a higher calling.

So, now that you've read a brief introduction on what this book is about, let's get through the informational pages, and then dive right in to the Ministry Study Curriculum, that is designed to help you discover and learn why the last thing a mature Christian needs is another Bible Study, if you haven't put into practice what you've been in class learning all these years. Let's get started...

<u>A personal note to Preachers, Reverends, Pastors, Priests & Bishops</u>

I'm writing a book on this next statement, but I'll touch on it briefly:

When did people that preach on Sunday start the tradition of taking off on Monday? Where can you come to work on the first day, then week after week take off the second day and expect to still have a job on the third? And where can you work just a few hours one day, and take off the next? Temp job, yes. Church...NO!

If you're wondering why members of your congregation are coming to church on Sunday but doing nothing on Monday, it could very well be because you're setting the example for them to do so.

Again, I'm working on a book on the subject, but I wanted to take this time and space to give you a glimpse so you may start thinking about where and how you fell into this tradition in the hopes that you'll break it. God Bless.

Church On Sunday | Nothing On Monday

Chapter One

WHAT IS CHURCH

"If I be lifted up from the Earth, I'll draw all men unto me."

John 12:32

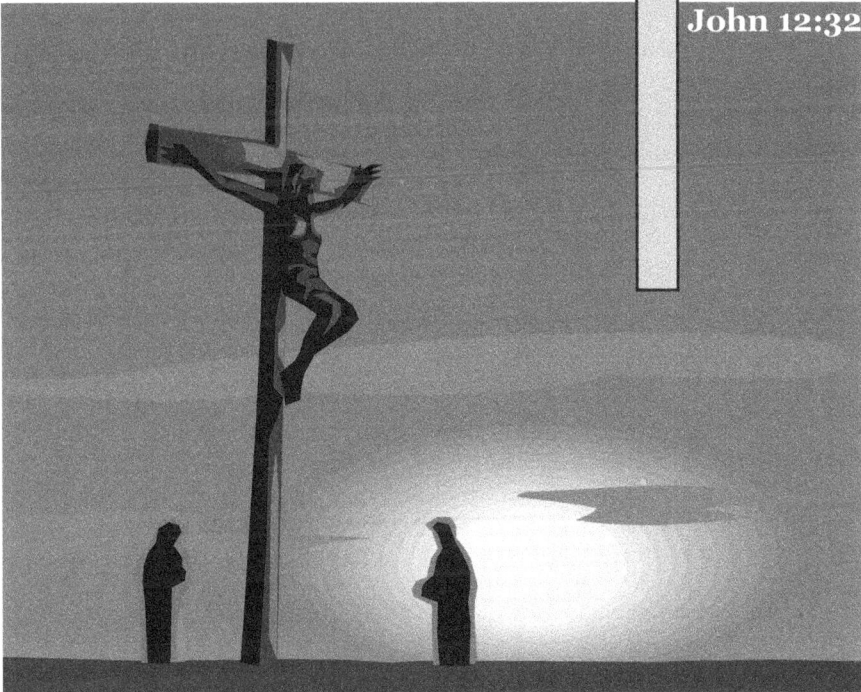

HISTORY OF THE CHRISTIAN CHURCH

Over 2000 years ago, **Our Lord and Savior Jesus Christ** established 'The Church'. Even though there are pastors, priests and bishop's who preside over 'the local church', **Jesus Christ** is both the head of 'the local church' and 'The Church'. And there is a distinct difference between the local church that people pastor, and The Church. Let me explain very briefly. When people surrender their lives to Christ, they join through the local church, but they are part of The Church, which Jesus will come back to harvest soon for the Kingdom of God.

THE LOCAL CHURCH

The local church is intended to be a sanctuary for worship. It is designed to be a hospital for the spiritually sick. It is meant to be a pillar in every community. **The local church** can be anywhere. It does not have to be in a physical building. **The local church** is made up of two or more people gathered together in the name of Jesus. They are called a congregation.

Members of the local church are considered the Body of Christ. And because there is a body, there is also a head, which is Christ. Most **local churches** operate in physical buildings where members of the congregation assemble to worship God, fellowship with each other and hear God's Word preached into our hearing regularly.

The local church operates under separation and autonomy from the government. It governs itself but is guided and held accountable for its actions by Jesus Christ, through His Holy Spirit.

Members of **the local church** serve as volunteers or in various paid positions to handle daily operations. **The local church** operates from Earth to Heaven. Exists here on Earth. Has many branches called churches. Has many denominations. Has many shepherds.

THE CHURCH

The Church is the Kingdom of God. It is Universal. Global. It operates from Heaven to Earth. Exists in Heaven and on Earth. Has One Shepherd, which is Jesus Christ. The Bible gives a clear indication of the authority of The Church over the local church in Psalm 127:1, which says, "Except the Lord (The Church) build the house (the local church), they labor in vain that build it."

In John 15:5, this authority is further identified and confirmed by declaring, "I am the Vine, you are the branches. If you remain in me and I in you, you will bear much fruit; apart from me you can do nothing." And continues to warn the local church leaders of the consequences of separating themselves from His will and authority. This history is an amazing relationship and exists with Jesus being the Founder and Chairman of the Board, and local pastors, priests, and bishops serving as CEOs.

The local church has full power and authority 'as a branch' to act on behalf of 'The Vine' as long as it remains connected to The Vine. Its purpose and mission must remain the same as originally established over 2000 years ago by The Vine. It must be ready in season and out of season, meaning when it feels like it, and when it doesn't, when it's popular, and when it isn't, to be a steadfast and unmovable representative of The Vine.

The local church ushers in new members to **The Church** so they can become part of the Kingdom of God, and work on becoming a righteous person, so they can spend eternity in Heaven with God, Jesus, the Holy Spirit, countless Angels, and many of the people you know, and meet along life's journey. Although, some of the people you know and meet along the way will not make it to Heaven. And part of the reason I wrote this book is to help Christians understand what can prevent them from getting there, such as settling into the tradition of church on Sunday and nothing on Monday.

This is a very dangerous routine that many Christians fall into, not knowing that it can and may prevent you from getting to Heaven.

How?

Because we can attend all the church services we want. Praise, sing, shout, pray, dance, and shout Hallelujah all we want. But if we never allow ourselves to be used by God in one of these areas of ministry such as feeding the hungry, clothing the naked, visiting the sick, helping strangers, ministering to prisoners, or helping to care for widows and orphans, all those church services and sermons will mean absolutely nothing.

HISTORY OF THE CHRISTIAN CHURCH

It's a simple concept.

FAITH (church) WITHOUT WORKS (ministry) is dead.

R
E
M
I
N
D
E
R

James 2:26

THE POLITICAL
& THE SOCIAL

Politics play a very important role in the church. 2000 years ago, there was no physical building where Christians could go and worship. Christians were persecuted for their faith so they had church mostly in their homes. Jesus established the church and left it in our hands so we would carry on the church and the ministry He started while He was here. 2000 years later, amazingly, the politics haven't changed. We are still being persecuted for our faith. And today, just like then, we are to campaign and cast our vote for Jesus, so others will cast their vote for Him because others are voting against Him.

Politics even plays an important role in the churches of today. In most churches I've ever been to, there is a political hierarchy and a social hierarchy. The political group consists of the Pastor, the deacons, other officers in the church, etc. They administrate, govern, teach and operate the church. **The social** groups, for example, consists of members who have been there the longest, those who have the most money, known each other the longest, etc. Within both the political and the social groups, as shown by Apostle Paul in most of his Epistles to the churches, you will hear, feel and experience things you won't like. Stay committed, don't get discouraged, keep reading, hearing, studying and doing what the Bible says, and most of all keep going and don't get weary (Galatians 6:9).

The social group often works against what the political group is trying to accomplish in the church. Just remember, you are there to praise and worship God, not people. Do what God has called you to do and leave everything else up to God.

Jesus has a mission for His ministry, His plan is always perfect, and His word can not come back to Him void. It will accomplish what He says it will, regardless of who opposes it.

THE POLITICAL AND THE SOCIAL

The Church Has Political and Social Aspects that are bigger than you and me. But Jesus is greater than all.

R E M I N D E R

ORGANIZATION OF THE CHRISTIAN CHURCH

Some churches have different titles and names for their leadership. However, in most Christian and other denominational churches, an organizational structure exists.

- **Pastor/Bishop** is the shepherd and overseer of the church.
- **Deacons** are men who serve the Pastor and the church.
- **Trustees** handle the fiscal management of the church.
- **Auxiliaries** or Committees manage different aspects of the church such as programs, events, fundraising, etc. Many churches call these ministries, but they rarely function as such.

Organization is needed to make sure everything is done decently and in order. Church organization is scriptural. Apostle Paul wrote about it in many Epistles.

There is **no perfect church**. So if you are looking for one, stop. It doesn't exist. Why? Because a church is made up of imperfect people. People who have flaws, issues, and other things you may or may not like. They are people just like you. The hope is, that while they are a member of the local church, through and by the process of surrender, confession, repentance, and forgiveness, they will be delivered from their issues. The same can be true for you.

There is no perfect church, but church done decently and in order can be a warm, loving, spirit-filled, happy, healthy, growing, nurturing, and inviting place that people will want to come and become a part of.

Again, the local church is simply the place that you join to be part of The Church, which Jesus Christ will soon return to harvest.

If you're not a member of a church, you have no chance of being saved, when Jesus returns.

ORGANIZATION OF THE CHRISTIAN CHURCH

There is no perfect church. So if you're looking for one, stop.

Because it doesn't exist.

R E M I N D E R

CHURCH
AND MINISTRY

Ephesians 2:10 says, "We are God's workmanship. Created in Christ Jesus to do good works, which God prepared in advance for us to do." Have you asked yourself what those 'good works' are? And have you wondered if they're prepared in advance for us, where are they?

The responsibility of every Christian is to learn the difference between church and ministry, and why we can't have one without the other, we must do both. Most Christians are used to just having church on Sunday, then doing nothing on Monday or the rest of the week, except Bible study on Wednesday nights. This man-made tradition has stood as the glass ceiling over the growth of many Christians for many decades. Our focus must be to break through that barrier.

Faith without works is dead, so we cannot just have church on Sunday, and not do the ministry work described in Matthew 25:35-36 starting on Monday, and through the rest of the week.

This scripture shows several aspects of ministry that are mandatory for every Christian to do in order to earn entrance to Heaven. Not all, just one of them. It helps strengthen our walk with Christ and strengthens us to help others do the same. This is what ministry work is, and Jesus put it in plain and simple terms so we'd understand.

The church is a hospital for the sick.

Ministry is the work Christians do to bring the sick to the hospital.

52 Weeks of Sunday School and Bible Study every year trains us.

Trains us to do what? To serve in church, and to work in ministry.

CHURCH AND MINISTRY

Church
shows our faith.
Ministry
shows our works.

R E M I N D E R

We cannot have one
without the other.

THE MISSION OF CHURCH

When Jesus established the church, His mission was to make it a place of **worship**, a place for the saints to come back and give praise reports on what they witnessed, and a place to teach others how to carry on the **work** that He started. Many churches have either lost their way, don't know the mission, or don't understand it. The ministry of Jesus is what established the church. His ministry included:

CHURCH - (a hospital for the sick)

Preaching

Anointing

Reaching

Teaching

MINISTRY - (work Christians do to bring the sick to the hospital)

Feed the hungry

Clothe the naked

Visit the sick

Minister to prisoners

Help strangers

Take care of widows

Spend time with orphans

Without these two things in place (church AND ministry) it is not a church that is continuing the ministry of Jesus Christ.

The mission is simple. No matter what we call it, it remains the same to this day: Win souls. Reach the lost. Feed His sheep. Help those who backslide, find their way home. Get people ready for Heaven. The list goes on and on. And somewhere, you fit into the structure of the local church, and the ministry. Because God, through His Holy Spirit, placed gifts inside you coupled with the passion to use them.

HISTORY OF THE CHRISTIAN CHURCH

R
E
M
I
N
D
E
R

We cannot have worship without doing the work.

CLUBS NOT CHURCHES

Some churches have lost their way because they've abandoned the mission and ministry of Jesus as it relates to church growth. They are content with just staying the way they are. Such churches are not really churches. They are actually social clubs trying to disguise themselves as a church. They are full of cliques and factions, and gossip, etc. They do church on Sunday, nothing on Monday.

Such churches are not difficult to spot. They have few youth and fewer new members. They are very weak in both these areas, and have no effort to grow in either area. Without a ministry for youth and new members, churches would cease to operate.

Other churches like this have abandoned the mission and ministry of Jesus to be worship centers for corporate types and are easy to identify. Most of the members are ages 30-60, upper middle class, very wealthy, and anyone who doesn't look like them, act like them, live where they live, work where they work, earn as much as they do, are not welcome. Instead of living out Matthew 25:35-36, they'd rather collect lots of money to donate so other people can do it.

In direct contrast to such churches, the church founded by Jesus Christ includes people from all walks of life, age, is evidenced by growth, is cultural, has rich and poor, and those in between, is diverse and operates by church worship and ministry work.

Again, there are many social clubs trying to disguise themselves as churches. Most of the leaders are the only ones who benefit. There are no morals, or foundation in Christ. And often, there is more sin being committed under the surface than in any other place on Earth. They only grow when they can find, lure, or deceive people into thinking they are something they are not. And there are many indicators and warning signs.

CLUBS NOT CHURCHES

Without Growth in the form of helping to save souls the Mission of the Church is already lost.

R E M I N D E R

MONEY NOT MINISTRY

Some churches have walked away from the mission and ministry of Jesus altogether. Their sole purpose is to make money. They do church on Sunday, nothing on Monday. Two Biblical examples are:

(1) Simon the sorcerer

(2) A slave girl was possessed with a spirit that predicted the future.

In the first example (Acts 8:9-24) a sorcerer named Simon, "amazed all the people of Samaria. He boasted that he was someone great, and all the people, both high and low, gave him their attention and exclaimed, 'This man is the divine power known as the Great Power.' They followed him because he had amazed them with his magic." When Phillip preached to them, not only did the people believe in Jesus, they were baptized. Even Simon himself, believed and was baptized. But Simon's true motive was revealed when he asked Phillip to sell him the power of the Holy Spirit so he could lay hands on the people. Some churches are following such men whose sole purpose is to make their own name great so lots of people will follow them and pay them.

In the second example (Acts 16:16-20) a slave girl was possessed with a spirit who could predict the future. She earned a great deal of money for her owners by fortune-telling. Paul cleansed her of the spirit and when the owners found out, they put him in jail.

Remember what Jesus said in John 15, He is the Vine, churches are the branches. Apart from Him we can do nothing. Branches that do not remain in Him are thrown away, withered, thrown into the fire, burned.

Unfortunately, the world is not without church leaders who have fallen into this trap. I've done a study on them the past few years, and wrote about the results in a book titled: *Pastors Are Not Perfect*.

MONEY NOT MINISTRY

REMINDER

If Money is the Mission and not Ministry, Churches have already missed the mark.

MEGA-CENTER NOT MISSION

Some churches have walked away from the mission and ministry of Jesus altogether, and their purpose is building a large membership. They do church on Sunday, nothing on Monday.

There are many churches with large memberships that continue to follow the mission and ministry of Jesus and through Him, are having a major impact on their immediate community, city, state, nation and globe. Such churches have people that are passionate about the mission and ministry of Jesus and understand that they can't just have church and not do ministry work such as feeding the hungry, clothing the naked, visiting the sick, ministering to prisoners, helping strangers, taking care of widows, and spending time with orphans.

But the churches with large memberships who have abandoned the mission of Jesus have no active ministry effort. They believe their ministry is the church. There is no effort to feed the hungry, visit the sick, minister to prisoners, help strangers, take care of widows, spend time with orphans, or have an impact on their immediate community, their city, state, nation, or globe. They exist to have church, nothing more.

Such churches are mega-centers full of people with no passion, no purpose and no works. Such churches are also known for preaching watered-down versions of the Gospel of Jesus Christ. This is what I call the vegetable diet. It always keeps the people coming back for more because they never receive meat or a full meal. Thank God that Jesus will separate the sheep from the goats when He returns.

MEGA-CENTER NOT MINISTRY

REMINDER

If Mega-Center is the mission the clear indication is that there is no Ministry.

CHAPTER ONE

R
E History of the Christian Church
C The Political and the Social
A
P Organization of the Church

Church and Ministry

The Mission of Church

Clubs Not Churches

Money Not Ministry

Mega Center Not Mission

Chapter Two

LEVELS OF CHURCH

"But solid food is for the mature, who by constant use have trained themselves to distinguish good from evil."

Hebrews 5:14

Church Level Chart

New Members

New members should be given a "new member packet" that contains: Church History, Info on the Pastor, Leadership, Mission, Services, Covenant, Beliefs, Auxiliaries, current Membership, Tithing, Baptism, Communion, Sunday School, Bible Study, Vacation Bible School, Weddings, Funerals, Dedications, Youth, Choirs, Website, Newsletters, any Television Outreach, Vision, Needs, Mission Work, Transportation, etc.

Kindergarten

Service in the Church

At this level, new members begin to worship, attend church services, participate in Bible studies, come to prayer meetings, show up for Sunday school. This is where we should learn how to worship God, how to pray, how to read the Bible, and learn what it means to walk with Christ and receive instruction on what our role is in the Body of Christ. This is just like elementary school.

Elementary

Serving in the Church

At this level we should encourage members to start serving on internal ministries. We should learn how to help fund raise, do strategic planning, create budgets; a brief list of internal ministries members can serve on include: Pastoral, Deacons, Deaconess, Trustees, Education, Ushers, Choir, Men, Women, Youth, Stewardship, Missions, Food & Clothing, Prison, Evangelism Cultural, Communications, Nominating, Benevolence, Events, Television, Technology, and any others that may be needed.

Junior High

Leadership in the Church

At this level, we serve in leadership roles on the internal ministries. We are the chairpersons. We should be the teachers of adult Sunday school. The Superintendent of Education. The Deacon chairperson. The head Deaconess. The Chair of the Trustees. By now, we should have grown enough to be in the leadership capacity within the church and should be trusted enough to carry out those duties effectively. We should be prepared for graduating to the next level, which is serving outside the church in ministry.

Senior High

Serving outside the Church

This is what ministry work is all about. And the reason for this book. This is where you take all the training you've received in Sunday school, church, and Bible study, and apply it throughout the week. It is taken directly from Matthew 25: 31-46 and includes feeding the hungry, clothing the naked, visiting the sick, ministering to prisoners, helping strangers, taking care of widows, and spending time with orphans. It is what Jesus said is a MUST for us to get into Heaven.

After Graduation

Levels Of Church

Levels of church are designed to help members grow from new creatures drinking milk, to mature Christians, feasting on the meat of God's Word. The following structure should be in place regardless of the church doctrine or its denomination. The first four levels are 'church', the fifth level is considered 'ministry'.

LEVEL ONE:

NEW MEMBERS

LEVEL TWO:

SERVICE IN THE CHURCH

LEVEL THREE:

SERVING IN THE CHURCH

LEVEL FOUR:

LEADERSHIP IN THE CHURCH

LEVEL FIVE:

SERVING OUTSIDE THE CHURCH

On the next few pages, I will identify and discuss what should happen at each of these levels. It's important because many Christians who could be effective leaders get stuck at level three, and even more become content with being at level four because they're "in charge" of something. But it is the duty of every Christian to bear fruit at level five, by serving in a Ministry outside the church. Each level unto itself, is as important as the next.

Level One
New Members

New members should be welcomed with open, loving, non-judgemental arms, as if it were the first day of Kindergarten. They are probably joining the church looking for God, and a relationship with Jesus. People who recently arrived at the church as new members should not be given the responsibility of welcoming other new members. The responsibility of welcoming new members should be given to seasoned members with warmth, maturity, and who know more about the church than a new member.

New members should be required to take a 'new member class' so they can learn about the church they've joined. The class should be taught by someone familiar with and active in every aspect of the church. It should be taught by someone in church leadership. The curriculum should come directly from a combination of material most important to helping new members adjust to their new life in Christ. Such as salvation, surrender, confession, repentance, redemption by the blood of Jesus, forgiveness, and transformation. Here is where we drink milk.

New members should be given a "new member packet" that contains: Church History, the Pastor and other Leadership; the Mission, Church Services, the Covenant, Beliefs, and Auxiliaries; Church Membership, Tithing, Baptism, Communion, Sunday School, Bible Study, and Vacation Bible School; Weddings, Funerals, and Dedications, Youth, Choirs, Website, Newsletters, TV Outreach; the Vision, Needs, Mission Work, and any Transportation. This information is vital in helping new members see where they can fit in.

For a guide on creating new members, see my book, *Welcome To Our Church: Guide To Creating New Member Packets.*

LEVEL 1: NEW MEMBERS (Kindergarten)	
Kindergarten is the place where every new member starts	R E M I N D E R

Level Two
Service In The Church

At this level, new members begin to worship, attend church services, participate in Bible studies, come to prayer meetings, show up for Sunday school. This is where we should learn how to worship God, how to pray, how to read the Bible, and learn what it means to walk with Christ and receive instruction on what our role is in the Body of Christ. This is just like elementary school.

At this level, we should learn about the Gospel of Jesus Christ, get to know the Disciples and their role. We should be introduced to Paul's conversion and deliverance. We should be taught the Old Testament, including the Tabernacle, the sacrifice of Tithing, and the prophets.

An in-depth class is needed at this level about the first church, and why it is important for Christians to make it through every level of church in order to be strong enough and mature enough to go and help establish churches in other parts of the world, especially in parts of the world where the name of Jesus is illegal, and where the name of Jesus has never been introduced.

Here is where we should be taught about of God's love, faith, fasting, deliverance, obedience, rules for living, what defiles us, and how testimony of where we came from can help others get to where we are. This level is elementary school for every Christian. We are still drinking milk, but there are a few cereal flakes (witness accounts and testimonies from the Bible) added to it to thicken it. These cereal flakes help prepare us to start eating meat.

LEVEL TWO: SERVICE IN THE CHURCH (Elementary)

R
E
M
I
N
D
E
R

Elementary School is where new members start learning about a few basic things pertaining to church.

Level Three
Serving In The Church

At this level, we should start getting into the meat of the Word. The scriptures should begin opening up to us and we should begin hearing and doing the word and growing stronger. We should learn that there is a war within us between our flesh and our spirit and the acts of our former sinful nature are detailed and we should show how we can use the fruit of the Spirit to overcome the acts of the sinful nature.

At this level we should encourage members to start serving on internal ministries. We should learn how to help fund raise, do strategic planning, create budgets, etc.

Here is where we should be encouraged to pray and ask God about which of the internal ministries He wants us to be involved in. Some people are not meant to serve on every internal ministry, just because they are a church member. "Specific gifts" are given by God through the Holy Spirit for the purpose of helping to build up the church.

For example, people who can preach and teach may not be gifted to serve on the internal ministry that is responsible for creating the annual budget. We should see where our gifts fit, and if it doesn't fit, don't force it. A brief list of internal ministries are: Pastoral, Deacons, Deaconess, Trustees, Education, Ushers, Choir, Men, Women, Youth, and other types such as Stewardship, Missions, Internal Food Shelf,

Prison, Evangelism, Cultural, Communications, Nominating, Benevolence, Events, Television, Technology, and any others that may be needed.

This is also a great place to conduct a survey to see what gifts members have and how they can best be used in the church.

LEVEL THREE: SERVING IN THE CHURCH (Junior High)

Junior High is where we begin using our gifts to start serving in the church.

R
E
M
I
N
D
E
R

Level Four
Leadership In The Church

At this level, we serve in leadership roles on the internal ministries. We are the chairpersons. We should be taught to start calling on the Holy Spirit to lead, guide, direct and order our steps. We walk in boldness and start calling out the enemies of Christ and wearing God's armor in our daily lives. We get on one accord with others who are doing the same. We start immediately exposing any strongholds attempting to creep back into our life and tearing down strongholds in the lives of others. Here we learn to serve God completely, in spirit and in truth and our prayer life is solidified.

We should be the teachers of adult Sunday school. The Superintendent of Education. The Deacon chairperson. The head Deaconess. The Chair of the Trustees. By now, we should have grown enough to be in the leadership capacity within the church and should be trusted enough to carry out those duties effectively.

We should be introduced to **ministries outside the church** (Food & Clothing, Visiting the Sick, Ministering to Prisoners, Helping Strangers, Taking Care of Widows and Orphans) and how to use our gifts in ministry. This is where we prepare to represent Jesus by serving on these ministries outside the church. And, as leaders, we should be introduced to 21st century ministries such as drug counseling, abstinence assistance, abortion advocacy, and others.

Most importantly, at this level, there should be a **formal graduation** to celebrate our years of church training and preparedness, by being awarded through licensing, a certificate to show others that we are ready to represent the church in ministry.

However, many Christians get stuck at this level because they are never taught that there is another level. So, Sundays and Wednesday year after year, they continue doing church on Sunday, nothing on Monday, never using the training they've received to this point.

LEVEL FOUR: LEADERSHIP IN THE CHURCH (Sr. High)

Senior High is when we use our gifts in leadership capacity within the church and prepare to graduate to minister outside the church.

R E M I N D E R

Level Five
Serving Outside The Church

In every school in the country, at this level, after graduation, students are either looking for work, or have found work. The same should be true with a Christian who has attended years of training in Sunday school and Bible Study.

Because of the training at levels 1-4, most Christians are more than ready to walk into their calling and go into ministry. But, many get stuck at "serving in the church" and never **graduate** to "serving outside the church." **After all, what did you think all that training was for? This is where we bear fruit for God. This is where we help build up and edify the Kingdom of God. This is where we help bring more people to God by introducing them to and ushering them into the church. This is where Jesus uses us to draw people unto Him.**

In John 15:16 Jesus said we did not choose Him, but He chose us and appointed us to go and bear fruit—fruit that will last. Romans 7:4-5 says more, and John 15:2 says even more.

It is for this reason that once we've completed new member's class, worshiped in countless church services, served inside the church, and been in leadership roles in the church, we are more than ready to go out and bear fruit in ministry!

Now, what could bearing fruit possibly mean? Simple. It's the work explained in Ephesians 2:10 that God prepared for us to do, Remember, faith without works is dead. In Matthew 25:35-36 Jesus explains the work, but most people miss the message: Verse 35 - "For I was hungry and you gave me something to eat." Verse 36 - "I needed clothes and you clothed me." "I was thirsty and you gave me something to drink.." "I was sick and you looked after me." "I was a stranger and you invited me in." "I was in prison and you came to visit me." The last two areas of work are explained by the brother of Jesus in the book of James, 1:27, which says: "To look after orphans and widows."

Everywhere on this planet, even though we have nations with an overabundance of money and power: There are always people who are hungry, there are always people who have no clothes, who are sick, have no homes, are in prison, in orphanages, widows. Why? Because this is the work God created for Christians to do, in order for us to learn to be like Christ.

LEVEL FIVE: SERVING OUTSIDE THE CHURCH	
What did you think all the Bible study and Sunday school was for?	R E M I N D E R

CHAPTER TWO

R
E
C
A
P

Church Level Chart

Levels of Church

Level One: New Members	[Kindergarten]
Level Two: Service In The Church	[Elementary]
Level Three: Serving In The Church	[Junior High]
Level Four: Leadership In The Church	[Senior High]
Level Five: Serving Outside The Church	[After Graduation]

Chapter Three

PREPARING FOR A MINISTRY STUDY

"Be ye doers of the word, and not hearers only, deceiving your own selves."

James 1:22

Going Beyond
Church & Bible Study

If you're like most average church members, who settle into the routine of going to Sunday school and church on Sunday, then Bible study on Wednesday, let me ask you a very serious question:

What is your understanding of what all that training you receive in Sunday school, sermons you listen to, and Bible Study you attend on Wednesday, is for?

Again, what did you think all the training was for?

Did it ever cross your mind, that God has a purpose in everything?

Has it ever made you think that there has to be something more than just going to Sunday school, church, and Bible study?

Has it ever been impressed upon your heart that there has to be something greater in God's purpose than what most churches are offering, providing, showing, teaching and giving their members?

If any of these questions hits you right at home, then you obviously have been thinking like so many others in that *Church on Sunday Nothing On Monday* is NOT the answer.

Going beyond Sunday school, church and Bible study takes 3 things:

1. Passion
2. Willingness
3. Commitment

PASSION

Many people have passion for something. And many people are passionate about something. But the kind of passion it takes to go beyond church and Bible study is different. It's different because in order to do it, you have to be:

- Passionate enough to 'break tradition'.
- Passionate enough to take the first step.
- Passionate enough not to care what others think.

If you don't have this kind of passion, find it, learn it, train yourself how to dig deep within yourself and bring it to the surface. Whatever you need to do, do it.

WILLINGNESS

If you're willing, God is able. God simply wants people who are willing to be representatives of His in different areas of Ministry. Period.

COMMITMENT

This is the most important of the three. Why? Because you can be full of passion, and more than willing, but if you never commit to taking the first step, you'll never go anywhere. And, you must also be willing to commit to continuing to take steps to go somewhere and help others. Remember, ministry work is NOT about you.

Showing Your Leadership The Need To Minister

Sheep can't lead sheep. Therefore, it takes a shepherd to show the flock where to go, and what to do when they get there.

Jesus set the standard, gave many examples, but one I will call upon to remind you is in Mark 6: starting at verse 7. Jesus, who had trained His Disciples, knew after 3 years, that they were more than ready to go out on their own, and put into practice, what He had taught them.

Unfortunately, sitting in most of the churches around the country right now, are members of many congregations that have been sitting in the pews and classrooms, receiving the same training over and over and over and over again, year after year, without ever being told it's time to go put what they've been taught into practice.

Three years. Not five. Not ten. And definitely not twenty or thirty. But again, sheep can't lead sheep. So if the shepherd does not tell the sheep that it's time to go, anoint them, AND open the gate for them to do so, they will stay right where they are comfortable. Next to the shepherd. This is truly a waste. It's a waste of teaching, training, talent, tools, testimony, and time.

What good is it to teach Sunday and Wednesday, year after year, if they're never going to use it, or you don't tell them how?

SHEPHERD

As a shepherd, it is your job, your duty, your responsibility to do what God has placed in your authority to do. **Once you've trained members, send them out to minister**. Here's a reality check. If you fail to do this, it is my opinion that you are responsible for them still sitting in your face five years, ten years, twenty years and even thirty years 'after' you should have pushed them out the door.

SHEEP

If you're a sheep, (that means church member), and you've been taught, trained, and shown how to go and DO God's word, but you're still sitting in the pews and classrooms HEARING God's word, here's your reality check. God called you. He used the church leaders to train you. He used the Holy Spirit to place gifts in you. And, He placed passion for something inside you to give you an assignment, place, and purpose to go and be His vessel on the battlefield.

So, if you're still sitting in the pews and classrooms because you've gotten so comfortable that you don't want to let yourself be used by God to go out and represent Him in the mission fields, then you are less than a sheep, you are actually a selfish sinner.

Sheep graze in the goodness of God's green pasture. They share in that goodness with other sheep. But selfish sinners want things to themselves, by themselves, for themselves. Rarely do they hear or heed the words 'it's not about you.' Remember 'Simon the Sorcerer.'

YOUR LEADERSHIP

If you're a Pastor, Priest, or Bishop, you have leadership under you. It can be one person, ten, or a hundred, this statement applies to all of them. If you're allowing the church leaders that are under you, to sit under you for more than three years without moving them on to minister, including and not limited to their own ministries, in my opinion, you are keeping them, and other members from growing. How? Simple. If you allow one person to occupy the same position under you year after year after year, what about other members who may be called and gifted to walk into that position? <u>Members are supposed to grow and go</u>! They are supposed to be trained within your church to go and minister outside the church; be taught to plant churches and anointed by you, to walk into their own ministries.

As a shepherd, you are the leader. Do you honestly think it's right for you to be leading the same members year after year? Or should it be that you anoint, elevate, and graduate them on to the next level, so you can usher in the next class of future leaders? You know right from wrong. And even if you think, say, or deny you don't, JESUS set the example, so use His teachings if you don't have your own, to teach, train, and show, then let them go!

The curriculum provided in this book is designed for you to start a Ministry Class in addition to your Bible Class. Why? Because there are members sitting in your pews who have learned more than enough and been there long enough to be elevated to the next level.

Using just **one of** these basic ministry activities, showing those in leadership under you the need to minister is quite simple. How? If you don't know, here you go, using feed the hungry as an example.

FEED THE HUNGRY

Call a meeting with your leaders, and take them to a shelter to serve food to those in the line to get meals. If there is no shelter near you, show them how to start a food shelf in your own church. And, go door to door in your own community to find out who needs food. The curriculum will take you in depth, but here are the other basic ministry functions that JESUS Himself established.

CLOTHE THE NAKED

VISIT THE SICK

MINISTER TO PRISONERS

HELP STRANGERS

TAKE CARE OF WIDOWS

SPEND TIME WITH ORPHANS

Again, 'one of these things' qualifies as doing it unto Jesus Himself. Showing the leaders that serve under you how to GO out and minister to others through protocol JESUS established, is Biblical and Basic. By the word basic, I mean just that. It's basic training. Training for what? For the immeasurable amount of other problems your ministers will eventually come across out on the battlefield and in the mission field.

The foundation Jesus laid for us, still serves as the basis and the basics for every church member to learn how to become more like Christ. Without one of these things on our schedule as a regular activity, we cannot hope to ever earn a place in the line with other sheep who will be waiting to go to Heaven. Instead, anyone who ignores this vital part of church, worship, and honoring God, will find themselves in line with goats, with hell being their destination.

I REFUSE TO GO TO HELL on the basis of missing the basics. And you, Mr. or Ms. Christian, should say the same.

YOU, Mr. or Ms. Shepherd, SHOULD REFUSE TO GO TO HELL on the basis of not teaching your leaders, and other members of your congregation destined to be leaders, how to avoid the goat line.

We must be DOERS of God's word not HEARERS only. And doing ministry work is the only way to make sure that happens.

	CHAPTER THREE
R E C A P	Going Beyond Church and Bible Study
	Showing Your Leadership The Need To Minister

Chapter Four

THE MINISTRY CLASS CURRICULUM

"I tell you the truth, whatever you did for one of the least of these brothers of mine, you did for me."

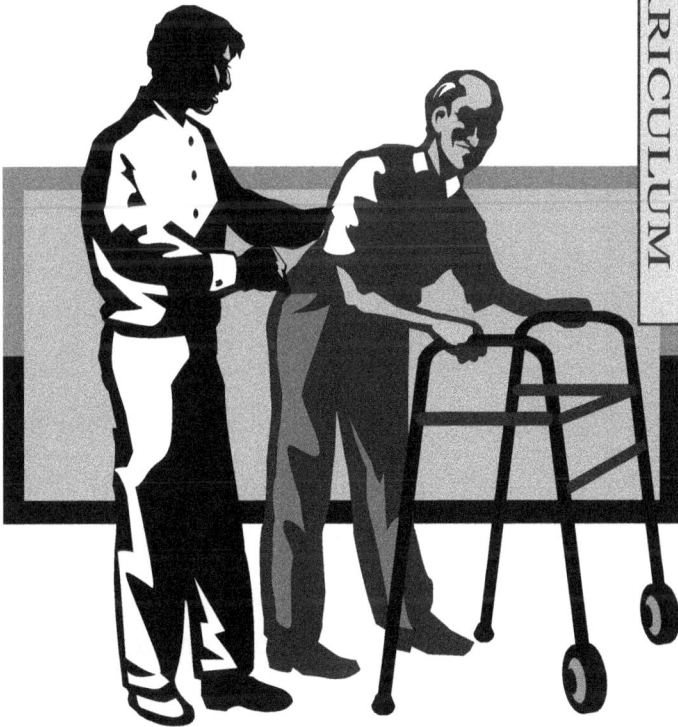

**Matthew
25:40**

The Sacrifice Of Time

In my book titled, *"Transform Your Schedule Transform Your Life"* the introduction points out that if you're anything like the average Christian, you drive to work, spend most of the day at work, drive home, eat, then settle in front of the TV or the Internet, waiting to go to bed to wake up the next morning and do it all over again.

In the book, I point out that this schedule is NOT ok for Christians.

Why? Because where does God fit into a schedule like that? Again, taking from the pages of the book I mention that without knowing you I can hear you respond by saying, you go to church on Sunday and Bible study on Wednesday, and possibly even Sunday school, thinking all the time that this is enough. IT ISN'T.

All throughout this book, *Church On Sunday Nothing On Monday*, I continue to reiterate that Jesus did NOT leave His home in Glory, to come to Earth, train us, get beaten for us, shed His blood for us, die for us, raise up from the dead for us, took the keys to death and hell for us, paid the penalty of sin for us to get up each day just to go work on someone else's worldly agenda and vision.

Jesus sacrificed His life for us to follow through on <u>His mission</u>, continue <u>His ministry</u>, and become members of <u>His Kingdom</u>.

Sacrificing time to do ministry work starts with being constantly and consistently reminded of certain things. Those things are:

- *You are a willing vessel*
- *You are a willing servant*
- *You are a living witness*
- *You are a living sacrifice*

What I mean by 'constantly' and 'consistently' reminded means doing everything you can to make yourself see these four statements all over your house, in your car, in your bathroom, in your kitchen, in your bedroom, on your refrigerator and near your washer and dryer. Post notes or whatever you need to and place reminders that you can physically see to help you remember your role in ministry.

While it should be obvious, I'll tell you why I left out two important places. What places?

- *In your wallet or purse*
- *In your Bible*

I left these two out because they are often in battle with each other. And I don't want you to be forced to choose between one or the other just to be reminded of which one is most important. If you don't already know the answer to that, then we have some very serious work to do, long before we get started on this Curriculum.

FIRST

In order to be successful sacrificing your time to GO and DO ministry work, you must be **willing**. If you're not willing, and you start doing this work, it will be laborious to you, you will grow tired of it, you will complain, grumble, and find every excuse in the book why you can't make it this day or the next. Forgetting that it's not about you. God wants you to be willing, so He can show you that He is able.

SECOND

Next, you have to have a heart to **serve**. Remember the story in the Bible where Jesus was about to feed thousands of people, and the Disciples, basically objected, asking Him to send the people away to get their own food. Jesus knew He could easily feed the people, but He wanted the Disciples to 'want' to feed the people. If you don't have the heart of a servant, ministry work will be difficult for you.

THIRD

You must be open to showing yourself as a living **witness** of how good God has been in your life by sharing your testimony with those you meet while doing ministry work. Remember, it's not about you. Your testimony is what can give people hope and inspiration to carry on when they are going through tough times and rough patches. God brought you through, and He can do the same for them too.

FOURTH

You must let go of the things of this world so you can be a **sacrifice** for God. This means giving up your wants and desires in order to let God use you to represent Him as a living sacrifice. And the only way this will work is if HIS TIME becomes more important than yours.

HIS TIME must be more important than checking your email.
HIS TIME must be more important that updating a status.
HIS TIME must be more important than your spouse.
HIS TIME must be more important than yourself.

God's time must take precedent over any and everything in your day. If it isn't, and you can't make the sacrifice to make it that way, ministry work will be tedious for you.

- *It will feel like work, rather than willingness.*
- *It will feel like labor rather than servitude.*
- *It will feel like wandering, rather than witnessing.*
- *It will feel selfish, rather than a sacrifice.*

So, if you can't get your mind and heart around these four components of ministry work, you may never be able to make your body want to go along for the ride. I say this because just sacrificing your time isn't all of it. Your feet, legs, arms, and other parts of you have to be just as willing to go along. Without them in compliance, and in a mode of willingness the same as your mind, your own body will do its best to place hurdles in your health to keep you from going to the places where God wants you go, to represent Him.

Setting A Schedule

Teaching yourself or leaders in your church that are under your care and tutelage, how to GO and DO God's word in the mission field and on the battlefield by doing ministry work, means you must lead by example. If you're the shepherd, and you haven't **done** what you are telling those under you they should **do**, you're likely not to get the response necessary to carry out the request. Jesus paved the way by showing the Disciples 'how' to do before He ever gave them the assignment to go and do. He led by example.

Setting a schedule to go and do ministry work is simple, once you get started. The hardest part to just about anything that requires a sacrifice of time and commitment, is getting started. Once you get started, ministry work will become more and more fulfilling. Taking the steps needed to get there will become easier. Moving everything and everyone else out of your way on the day(s) you choose to minister, will be done without hesitation and for HIS glory. There is no greater accomplishment in life, than to know you are walking in God will and in God's purpose for your life.

The following pages contain a sample and suggested schedule in calendar form, for you to consider doing '**one of**' these ministry activities. For a more in-depth look at setting a schedule, please read the chapter *Transforming Your Schedule* in my book titled, *Transform Your Schedule Transform Your Life.*

There's nothing worse than going to church on Sunday and doing nothing on Monday or the rest of the week. So, for one hour every Monday, regardless of what hour you choose, stick to the schedule.

Again, Jesus says if you've done '**one of**' these ministry activities for others, it's as if you've done it unto Him.

Ministry On Mondays
Reach the lost in the streets and parks (week 1 and 5)
Help strangers locate housing (week 2 and 4)
Reach the lost on buses and bus stops (week 3)

What I Suggest
Load up a duffel bag or briefcase with tracts and booklets; make yourself available to answer any questions; And invite them to Bible study, because it's often easier than getting them to come to church.

Home On Mondays
After an hour on the street doing ministry, when you get home:
Watch Christian TV for 1-2 hours.
Read Matthew 10th chapter.

Monday	
Week 1	Reach the lost in the streets and parks Watch Christian TV for 1-2 hours; Read Matthew 10th chapter
Week 2	Volunteer at a local agency to help strangers find housing Watch Christian TV for 1-2 hours; Read Matthew 10th chapter
Week 3	Reach the lost on buses and bus stops Watch Christian TV for 1-2 hours; Read Matthew 10th chapter
Week 4	Volunteer at a local agency to help strangers find housing Watch Christian TV for 1-2 hours; Read Matthew 10th chapter
Week 5	Reach the lost in the streets and parks Watch Christian TV for 1-2 hours; Read Matthew 10th chapter

Now that you've gotten started, it gets easier for you to take the next step. Again, for one hour every Tuesday, regardless of what hour or time you choose, stick to the schedule.

REMINDER: Ministry work is NOT About you.

Ministry On Tuesdays

Visit the sick in nursing homes   (week 1 and 2)
Visit the sick in ICU and cancer units   (week 3 and 4)
Visit the sick in veterans homes   (week 5)

What I Suggest

Load up a backpack or briefcase up so you can hand out tracts and booklets; be available to answer questions; Pray with them, then read a scripture or passage that comes to heart; then sing a song or two. Remember Matthew 25:31-46, and James 2:14-16.

Home On Tuesdays

After spending an hour visiting the sick, when you get home:
Walk for 1-2 miles.
Watch Christian TV for 1-2 hours.

Tuesday	
Week 1	Visit the sick in nursing homes Walk for 1-2 miles; Watch Christian TV for 1-2 hours
Week 2	Visit the sick in nursing homes Walk for 1-2 miles; Watch Christian TV for 1-2 hours
Week 3	Visit the sick in ICU and cancer units Walk for 1-2 miles; Watch Christian TV for 1-2 hours
Week 4	Visit the sick in ICU and cancer units Walk for 1-2 miles; Watch Christian TV for 1-2 hours
Week 5	Visit the sick in veterans homes Walk for 1-2 miles; Watch Christian TV for 1-2 hours

Now it's mid-week. Congratulations for whatever day and time and hour you've chosen as your time to GO and DO ministry work to help others. If you've made the ultimate sacrifice of doing it for one hour every day, Hallelujah for completing Monday and Tuesday!

Wednesday is a day of study and learning; go to your church Bible study or other Christian classes, but stick to the schedule.

No Ministry On Wednesdays
Bible Study and/or other classes   (week 1 - 5)

What I Suggest
During the hour you would normally be doing ministry work, if you're not in classes anywhere, take a walk, maybe by the lake, spending alone time praying and giving God glory. In the evening, attend Bible study at a church, which normally starts at 6 or 7 p.m.

Home On Wednesdays
Clean the house and catch up on the laundry from Sunday, Monday & Tuesday. Listen to Christian Radio or Gospel / contemporary Christian music.

Wednesday	
Week 1	Walk for 1-2 miles; Bible study; Clean house, laundry, listen to Christian radio.
Week 2	Walk for 1-2 miles; Bible study; Clean house, laundry, listen to Christian radio.
Week 3	Walk for 1-2 miles; Bible study; Clean house, laundry, listen to Christian radio.
Week 4	Walk for 1-2 miles; Bible study; Clean house, laundry, listen to Christian radio.
Week 5	Walk for 1-2 miles; Bible study; Clean house, laundry, listen to Christian radio.

Two more days to go. Have you felt the difference yet? Has God sent anyone to you for help or advice? If He hasn't yet, keep watching. God knows where all of His resources are. And now that you've decided to let God use you, He will. Keep watch for Him to send others your way. And, continue to stick to the schedule.

Ministry On Thursdays

Feed the hungry   (week 1, 3, 5)
Clothe the naked   (week 2 and 4)

What I Suggest

(feeding) Volunteer at a homeless shelter in their food line; or, make about 25 bag lunches with a piece of fruit and a bottle of water; hand them out where the homeless hang out during the day;
(clothing) Go to a halfway house where men are coming home from prison; buy 1 or 2 of them clothes to work in. Hand out tracts & booklets; be available for questions.

Home On Thursdays

Walk for 1-2 miles.
Read Galatians 5:16-26.

Thursday	
Week 1	Feed the hungry in shelters or on the street Walk for 1-2 miles; Watch Christian TV for 1-2 hours
Week 2	Clothe the naked coming out of prisons Walk for 1-2 miles; Watch Christian TV for 1-2 hours
Week 3	Feed the hungry in shelters or on the street Walk for 1-2 miles; Watch Christian TV for 1-2 hours
Week 4	Clothe the naked coming out of prisons Walk for 1-2 miles; Watch Christian TV for 1-2 hours
Week 5	Feed the hungry in shelters or on the street Walk for 1-2 miles; Watch Christian TV for 1-2 hours

Faithful Friday. What kind of praise reports do you have to share at your church or with me? You can send me your praise reports to praisereports@LessonsForLifeBooks.com or share them with others on Blog.LessonsForLifeBooks.com. Remember to stay on schedule.

Ministry On Fridays

Send letters/newsletters to prisoners	(week 1)
Help widows/widowers with chores	(week 2)
Hand out material at halfway houses	(week 3)
Go read books at an orphanage	(week 4)
Help ex-prisoners locate housing and jobs	(week 5)

What I Suggest

(prisoners) I send letters/newsletters; (widows/widowers) Take them to get grocery; haircuts, mow lawns, shovel snow, rake leaves, play board games; (orphans) Read books at orphanages; be available for questions.

Home On Fridays

Walk for 1-2 miles.
Listen to Christian radio or Gospel / contemporary Christian music.

Friday	
Week 1	Send letters/newsletters to prisoners Walk for 1-2 miles; listen to Christian radio.
Week 2	Help widows/widows with chores Walk for 1-2 miles; listen to Christian radio.
Week 3	Hand out tracks/booklets at halfway houses Walk for 1-2 miles; listen to Christian radio.
Week 4	Go read books at an orphanage Walk for 1-2 miles; listen to Christian radio.
Week 5	Help ex-prisoners locate housing and jobs Walk for 1-2 miles; listen to Christian radio.

Anointing and Releasing Your Leadership

Throughout this book, I've urged you to treat the leaders that are serving under you as members of a class that 'you are expecting to graduate, elevate, anoint, and release, so they can move on to the next level. Otherwise, how else will you usher in the another class?

Many churches, and the shepherds of the flocks in those churches, forget, neglect, and often ignore this all important step.

Anointing and releasing your leadership is VITAL to their growth, and to your own. The leaders in your care have made it there through whatever means or method it took for them to get under you. How it happened does not matter. Jesus hand picked His twelve. He set the example. And in my humble opinion, the same standard should still be followed to this day by other shepherds.

But, in order to follow the example and standard Jesus set, you must be willing to teach those under you how to make the sacrifices necessary for them to learn what they need to with you, then take what you've taught them on to the next level.

When you have anointed and released your first 'graduating class' of leaders under you to GO and DO ministry work, your own growth will come through the experience of having successfully done so.

Again, treat those under you as if they are your students, trainees, or whatever you need to call them, but know that they are under you for a season, then you have to release them so they can GROW UP.

Here is a statement that you should type in large bold letters and place it somewhere in your pastoral office so you can see it regularly.

Some of the leaders you train will leave you to start their own churches and ministries, and some will stay to work in the ministry in your church.

Whichever the case, both benefit the Kingdom of God, which is the purpose for which you have trained them in the first place.

ANOINTING AND RELEASING YOUR LEADERSHIP

R
E
M
I
N
D
E
R

Jesus trained His Disciples for three years.

Then He released them to go work in the ministry.

You need to do the same.

Requiring and Expecting Praise Reports

Jesus trained His Disciples for three years. They shadowed Him with nearly everything He did, and accompanied Him almost everywhere He went. And when Jesus knew they were ready to GO and DO what He had trained them to do, He anointed and released them by giving them an assignment.

But it didn't end there.

Along with the assignment, He instructed them to return back to Him and REPORT what they had seen, witnessed, and experienced His power DO through them.

These praise reports are VITAL to the growth of those future leaders in training, as well as to other members of your congregation. Why? Because they are 'testimony' of the truth, goodness, and effectiveness of an immortal God's power and authority working in and through mortal men.

Once you've trained, anointed and prepared to release those who have served under you into their own churches or ministries, or even to represent your church outside the walls in an area of ministry, you should give them the assignment, but also REQUIRE them to follow through by returning to you from time to time to give a report.

You may ask why this is important, but I just explained it in terms as simple as I could. It is VITAL to you, future leaders under you, and to members of your congregation because the testimony serves as hope and inspiration to others.

Praise Reports from people you've trained also help you to be constantly reminded that your walk is NOT ABOUT YOU. God chose you to be the leader, shepherd, overseer of the flock under you. And as the watchman of their souls, you have been called, gifted, educated, trained, pruned, and are constantly fed to carry out the mission to which you have been assigned. And although the mission may sometimes seem impossible, praise reports are one sure way to be reminded that accepting the mission was the best decision.

REQUIRING AND EXPECTING PRAISE REPORTS

Praise Reports can help remind you that what you taught them is powerful and effective for the edification and uplifting of the saints the church and the ministry.

R
E
M
I
N
D
E
R

Preparing For Your
New Growth

In my book, *Welcome To Our Church: Guide To Creating New Member Packets*, I give specific instructions and templates to help churches prepare for new growth. This section is specifically for leaders you have trained, anointed, and released, for the purpose of them representing your church by doing ministry work.

When you send leaders out into the battlefield and on the mission field, one thing for sure is going to take place. Jesus will be lifted up.

And when that happens, He will draw men unto Him, by guiding them to your church. The Bible, in the book of Acts, often talks about how many people joined the church when Jesus was lifted up. So, let's briefly look at the numbers and how they can work for your growth at the local level, AND for the advancement of God's Kingdom.

- You are the Shepherd
- You have five leaders that you've trained, anointed, and released.
- Each leader is responsible for reaching one person per/month.
- In a year, sixty new souls will be added to God's Kingdom.

And, this is being done because of you being willing to train, graduate, anoint, and release those who were ready to go and represent God, Jesus, the Holy Spirit, the local church, and God's Kingdom.

This is just an example of how growth can happen. Not every period of membership enhancement will be as structured as this example.

Jesus draws.

We stand at the door with open arms.

People who are hurting both physically and spiritually will be drawn to Jesus through you and your leaders because they see Him in you. They will be seeking help in the spiritual hospital called your church. And because they will be expecting help when they get there, you need to be prepared to provide that help in whatever form is applicable to their individual and different and varying situations. Once they arrive, it is the love and passion and compassion of Jesus Christ that you must use to help keep them there.

PREPARING FOR YOUR NEW GROWTH

R
E
M
I
N
D
E
R

Growth will happen once you've sent them out and Jesus is lifted up, but you must be prepared to receive them when they arrive.

Feeding The Hungry

If you've attended Sunday school and Bible study for more than 3 years, you should be more than ready to move on to the next level.

Therefore, now that you've been trained, and you should have been through a graduation to celebrate your being ready to represent the church doing ministry work, there are a few options.

Jesus said that if we do **one of** these options to the least of His people, we've done it unto Him. I highly recommend participating in all of the ministries when you're first starting out, to get the experience, but settle into the one where your gifts and passion call you.

My passion for feeding the hungry comes from being homeless at one point in my life. So I know what it's like to be hungry. I suggest feeding people on the street, in food centers, serving lines, etc. I encourage buying hot food and handing it out; make bag lunches and hand those out; bake cookies and cakes and give those away.

This ministry goes hand in hand with clothing the naked. I normally feed the hungry on **Thursdays**. The next week, I'll clothe the naked. I participate in annual food and clothing drives and provide holiday meals and winter clothing to individuals and families. I meet so many people who are in need of just basic things to survive, it warms my heart when I can help.

The opening statement to this Feeding the Hungry section probably shocked you somewhat, because most likely no one has ever said these words to you, but in fact, you've read them, heard them, and probably studied them at some point, through reading about Jesus and the Disciples, but because it was never put in this context to you, you're still a bit shaken from the reality of what I just said. So, take some time to take it in, then, let's move on.

Now that you're in the role to represent the church in ministry, start a food drive and encourage the members of your church to pick up just one extra item each time they go to the store to give to the food drive. And stay on them. Call them if necessary. Get the kids in the family involved. They will often remember to bring the food bag to church more than the adults will. Be blessed in your work in ministry!

FEEDING THE HUNGRY

R
E
M
I
N
D
E
R

**There are many ways
to feed the hungry
when you have
a passion to do so.
Always remember to go out
in twos, in teams, together.**

Clothing The Naked

I'm repeating the following statement to help you understand the importance:

"If you've attended Sunday school and Bible study for more than 3 years, you should be more than ready to move on to the next level.

Therefore, now that you've been trained, and you should have been through a graduation to celebrate your being ready to represent the church doing ministry work, there are a few options.

*Jesus said that if we do **one of** these options to the least of His people, we've done it unto Him. I highly recommend participating in all of the ministries when you're first starting out, to get the experience, but settle into the one where your gifts and passion call you."*

Again, feeding the hungry goes hand in hand with clothing the naked. I normally do both on alternating **Thursdays**. One week, I'll feed the hungry. The next week, I'll clothe the naked.

I participate in annual clothing drives and provide winter clothing to individuals and families. And, I've learned many other ways to clothe those in need by just talking to and listening to their needs. For example, when inmates are just being released from prison, they rarely have more than a few items of clothing to come home with.

A way to help is to visit the halfway house with another member of your church (reminder: always go in twos, in teams, together), create a list of the residents and their needs. Some will need basic clothing such as something other than the 'blues' or 'oranges' they were forced to wear while incarcerated. Others will need clothes appropriate for job interviews, and/or to wear to work once they've landed the job.

There are numerous ways to help people get clothing applicable to their needs and situations. Families with children living in shelters come to mind, as well as single moms with kids, whose income from working only covers their rent and food, but leaves nothing for being able to keep the kids in clothing appropriate to wear to school.

Whatever the situation, ask God to show you where you are needed.

CLOTHING THE NAKED

REMINDER

Thrift stores are a great way to stock up on clothing for people who need it. Another way is to clean out your very own closet. When you give stuff away it makes room for more.

Visiting The Sick

In 1979, my dad became stricken with respiratory illness that had him bedridden and on oxygen. I cared for him until he went to the doctor escorted by my sister's father-in-law, Mr. Collie. Little did I know that would be the last time I saw my dad alive. He never came home from the doctor. He passed away November 24th, 1980.

Because of that experience, when I'm active in ministry work, and not taking a break to write more books, on **Tuesdays** each week I go into the hospitals, veterans homes, hospices, nursing homes and other care centers, to sing, pray, and minister to the sick. I give them Bibles if they want them and other spiritual material including copies of my books. Because I've been taught and trained many years, I'm prepared to answer most questions they may have. I bring caring, concern and hope to those suffering. I often take a few other people along with me so they can experience how God uses ordinary people that are willing vessels in extraordinary ways.

There are numerous ways to share the love of Jesus with the sick. Remember, those that are elderly, took care of us until we were able to take care of ourselves. Now it is our responsibility to reciprocate, and take care of them. Reading the Bible to someone sick, can have a healing effect. Or, visiting the Veterans Hospital to let the men and women of our armed forces know that someone cares about them and their families, makes a world of difference.

During my college years, a few years after my dad passed, I met a dentist named Hazel Phoenix, who lived on 72nd & Rhodes in Chicago. Her husband Fred, was stricken with a stroke. Because of the experience I had caring for my dad, I stepped right in and began taking care of Mr. Phoenix, while he was bedridden.

Mrs. Phoenix was grateful. I was Blessed. And Fred, had a smile that lit up the room every time I arrived to feed him, read to him, help him exercise, or just to change the bed linen he had soiled.

I took my wife to meet Ms. Phoenix the day I gave her a 24x36 pencil-drawn rendition I had done of the Chicago Skyline. The smile on Ms. Phoenix's face let me know she was well pleased. Simple sacrifices, lasting impact.

VISITING THE SICK

R E M I N D E R

I never knew I had a passion or even the compassion for visiting the sick until I was put in a position where I had to.

Allow yourself to be used and let God do the rest.

Minister To Prisoners

When doing ministry work outside the church, this is a specialized area of ministry to focus on. Having been incarcerated myself more than once, this ministry is close to my heart. Because of that passion, I <u>write letters of encouragement</u> to those still inside; <u>deliver Bibles, booklets and tracts</u>, to halfway houses and I'm prepared to answer any questions they may have.

On Fridays each week, again, when I'm not taking a break to write more books, I <u>go to halfway houses, county jails, court appointed group sessions</u>, etc. I often take a few other people along with me so they can witness and experience the truly awesome and wonderful things God does when He has a willing vessel to go and represent Him in the places most people wouldn't be caught dead in.

There are numerous opportunities to share the love of Jesus with those in prison. For example, I've designed a <u>database</u> that helps me keep up with each inmate God places in my path. I use the database to remind me to send birthday cards, etc. And, I publish a <u>newsletter</u> to mail out to them. And, I've developed the business plan for a project that hopefully someday will be a dynamic resource for <u>transitional housing for people being released from prison</u>. The project is called 'TransiHouse.' It's short for transitional housing but will also provide <u>ten essential life skills</u> that my research shows most prisoners are lacking before and upon release.

I started the project after being incarcerated myself and seeing firsthand how many people end up back in prison soon after being released, because of no stable housing, no support system, or any resources to teach them how to stay crime free.

You can learn more on this project in my book, *"How Are You Living: Ten Essentials Life Skills For Ex-Offenders"* which includes the TransiHouse business plan, flyer, and brochure. I've also inserted a list of resources for you to use in your prison ministry.

Again, this ministry is near and dear to my heart, and I still do almost everything I can to continue ministering to prisoners who are facing tough challenges both inside and out.

MINISTER TO PRISONERS

R
E
M
I
N
D
E
R

Prison ministry is a highly specialized area to work in.

It takes compassion but even before that, true forgiveness has to lay the foundation.

Helping Strangers

In representing your church doing ministry work, this option takes compassion. My compassion for helping strangers comes from the early 1980s when after my Dad passed, I found myself homeless for a short time. I was too proud to seek help, or tell anyone, including my own family.

I knew nothing about shelters. So, me and my high priced suits, oxford shirts, and florsheim shoes, slept on park benches in Grant Park. I will always remember how cold and lonely it felt sleeping on those benches. If it weren't for a ***stranger*** who saw me a few days in a row, and told me about the Pacific Garden Mission a few blocks away, I can only imagine what may have happened.

Because of the kindness of that stranger, on **Mondays**, when I'm not taking a break to write books, I spend time just going places where I know homeless people are, with the sole purpose of giving them resources that will help them locate short and long-term housing. In certain situations, mostly where kids are involved, I attempt to cover motel costs until I can find them other housing.

My compassion for helping strangers also comes from seeing so many others ignore people who are standing on street corners holding signs, and being passed by day after day by Christians who have the answer they are looking for, and the help they need, in Jesus.

My suggestion to you, as a member of the Body of Christ, is to have it in your heart to pack a bag lunch; buy a gift Bible from a discount store or Christian bookstore; and take an hour one day each week, to find someone holding a sign standing on the street by the freeway.

Your purpose for finding them is simple:

1. To learn and realize that their sign does not ask for money.
2. To share some natural food with them, through the bag lunch.
3. To give them the best gift you could possibly ever give, a Bible.
4. To introduce them to the place to find the answers they seek.
5. To let them know that someone understands what they truly need.

Treat this ministry *as if God Himself placed them there on that street to see how many Christians would stop to help.*

HELP STRANGERS

R E M I N D E R

Don't assume that someone holding a sign is asking for money.

You have exactly what they really need so give <u>Him</u>, to them.

Taking Care
Of Widows

As a willing vessel doing ministry work, you will notice that each of the ministries Jesus compelled us to work in never ends. There are always people in need, regardless of how much money or power countries and governments and rich people have. This is because God has ordained for certain people to be hungry, naked, sick, in prison, strangers, widowed, and orphaned.

Think about it. If none of these ministries existed, who would Christians minister to? God's word in Ephesians 2:10 is plain and simple. This is the 'work' God prepared in advance for us to do. And these are the people we are called to minister to.

As a willing vessel, you'll either have the compassion it takes to help widows and widowers, or it will certainly grow on you. After you see enough of them in need, it will start to affect you. I look at it this way: The elderly who have lost a loved one, can find that same love in you, when you share the love of Jesus that is in you, with them.

Another way I look at it is this: When we were younger, our parents raised us, fed us, clothed us, took care of us when we were sick, ministered to us when we were in prison (no matter what 'type' of bondage it was), so now it is time to do the same for them when they are older. This is called reciprocity, and this ministry requires it.

You can find your passion for taking care of widows and widowers quite easily. Spend time taking them to grocery shop, or to doctor's appointments; to get hair cuts, shovel their snow, rake their leaves, pull weeds, cut grass, or just hang out and play games like cards, checkers, chess or cribbage. Or, go watch a ball game together.

Just something as simple as sitting with them an hour a couple of days a week to watch their favorite show or the read and discuss the Good News of the Gospel of Jesus Christ, can have a lasting impact in their lives.

Those who are widows and widowers, whether they had their own kids or not, deserve our help and support when they become elderly, because it is the Biblical thing to do. So take time to make it happen.

TAKE CARE OF WIDOWS

R
E
M
I
N
D
E
R

Taking care of our elders when they get older is Biblical.

It is called reciprocity which is doing for them what they did for us.

Spending Time With Orphans

For me, this is the most difficult ministry to work in. Seeing a child without parents to care for them, is tough for me.

My parents passed when I was young. My mom passed when I was age 9. My dad passed when I was age 17. I felt abandoned. Left behind. Orphaned. These feelings not only surfaced, others did too. Such as anger and resentment. I knew nothing about death and the adults in my family never said a word.

Children who have no parents, whether from death, adoption, or a host of other reasons, typically all feel the same and ask themselves the same question: Why me?

As a willing vessel, your responsibility is NOT to answer that question. In fact, it's not even recommended that you try to answer. As difficult as it will probably be to refrain from trying to give an opinion of what has happened in their individual situation, keep the focus on Jesus, and let the Holy Spirit use you to minister the words needed to bring understanding, peace, and clarity to your conversation. On your journey of spending time with orphans, you may even meet kids who are waiting to be adopted. Word of advice: you cannot adopt them all. Because of the compassion in your heart, you will want to, but you cannot.

You can find your passion for spending time with orphans easily. Start by just going to orphanages and reading books. Spend time or just making your presence known there by hanging out and playing games, teaching them skills you have that can be passed on, or using your gifts to help them learn something new, that you can teach them how to do. Or, if and when allowed, watch a ball game together.

Something as simple as sitting with them an hour a couple of days a week to watch their favorite show or the read and discuss things they have questions about can have a lasting impact in their lives.

Kids, just want to be kids. And they want to be loved. You can help them be just that.

SPENDING TIME WITH ORPHANS

R E M I N D E R

Every child deserves love and a caring family. Whether you have kids or not you'll know how valuable this wonderful gift is when you see a child without parents.

CHAPTER FOUR

R E C A P

The Sacrifice Of TIme

Setting A Schedule

Anointing And Releasing Your Leadership

Requiring And Expecting Praise Reports

Preparing For Your Growth

Feeding The Hungry

Clothing The Naked

Visiting The Sick

Ministering To Prisoners

Helping Strangers

Taking Care Of Widows

Spending Time With Orphans

Chapter Five

VITAL NEW AREAS OF MINISTRY

"Now the Spirit speaketh expressly, that in the latter times some shall depart from the faith, giving heed to seducing spirits, and doctrines of devils."

1st Timothy 4:1

Ministering To Today's Problems

Even if you're new to ministry work, you're not new to things that take place in our society that I'm about to talk about in this section.

When Jesus established the church over 2000 years ago, there was prostitution, murders, prisoners, even homosexuals. Even though these issues existed back then, in today's society these and other areas are the reason for entire industries being developed such as Psychology. While there may not have been shrinks back then, they were needed. And because the problems of any society grow as time passes, so does the need for such practitioners.

Churches that confront and address such issues are likely very concerned about the well-being of its members. Why? Because I know numerous churches that are afraid to even consider the creation of ministries to address such issues. Those are churches I consider not truly following Christ, and certainly are dark ages in their thinking.

Jesus dealt with the issues of the sick, he dealt with the issues of those who needed lawyers, he dealt with the issues of prostitutes, and even the issues of adulterers. But his purpose was not to shun them, or pretend their issues didn't exist. He actually confronted their issues in the way that churches should today, by dealing with the root cause, which is sin.

The approach Jesus took was so radical and forward-thinking when dealing with people's issues, that many people were astonished, and didn't know how to respond to it. But what Jesus was doing was writing a blueprint for us, to first let us know that the issues exist, then to show us how to deal with them.

Since Jesus left, many more issues have surfaced but the approach still remains the same. What's missing? Churches willing to step up to the plate and deal with today's problems like Jesus did back then.

How would you feel being a member of a church where you constantly hear that the church is a hospital for the sick, but your church turned away people with problems from its triage because it's not equipped to handle them? I've experienced it, and it's no fun.

Many churches today do not realize that they are hospitals turning away patients, because they do not have the compassion it takes to deal with their issues or problems, or the patience to even address it. I'll go one step further and say that many churches also do not have the radical courage that Jesus had to step up, confront the issue, and take action to see that it is corrected, so the person can be delivered and heal.

There is no end-all list of problems that churches can work to create ministries, or support groups to address, but I've listed some of the basic ones here.

Some members sitting in the pews each and every Sunday:

- have kids who've run away
- have kids who've killed other kids
- are facing foreclosure, eviction or already homeless
- have major health issues such as HIV, AIDS or CANCER
- have spouses or family members who are incarcerated
- have pregnant teens
- have money, debt and credit problems
- have never healed from slavery and segregation
- are alcoholics and/or drug addicts
- are current or former prostitutes
- are homosexual
- still carry prejudice in their hearts
- have lost spouses and family members to wars
- are facing divorce or dealing with adultery
- are families that have been displaced from natural disasters
- have lost homes, businesses, and other things due to this economy
- have been physically, sexually, and/or emotionally abused

...and some of them are dealing with it sitting next to you in the pew.

There are a host of other common social problems that churches need to provide support for on top of the weekly 'make me feel good sermon' or sermonette. It isn't difficult to address these issues, but some churches are completely lacking in the professional or spiritual capacity to do so. Few, even want to, but certainly need to try.

Telling someone who's hurting that 'Jesus will fix it', or 'Prayer changes things', or 'Wait on the Lord', doesn't help much at all the moment you learn your spouse is cheating on you, especially if you're a new member. Churches have to become more actively involved in he lives of 'all' its members in order to be more responsive to their immediate and long-term needs, especially when they're in crisis.

I remember my own crisis when I received a knock on the door at 1:30a.m. in 2005, answered the door, and didn't return home for the next six months. At the door were officers and I was being arrested for violating a ten-year-old probation, by not paying off restitution that I had already paid 34K into, but had not paid the last 17K when I certainly had more than enough money and opportunity and time to do so. I was totally and completely in the wrong.

My wife and kids were left behind wondering what was happening, and unsure of what to do about the 5K in monthly bills I had been paying. They quickly faced eviction, and our church did nothing. We had been Tithe-paying members for 7 years; and I had been in leadership for 5. But one man, K.S., who I will always be grateful to, stepped up to help. We are no longer at that church. And I do my best to try and help other churches see how it can become better equipped to deal with the emergencies and issues of its members, even if just a support group. Not paying the restitution balance was my fault, but I believe churches have a responsibility to Christ to try and help its members, whenever they are in crisis.

My story is no different than many of the individuals and families I've seen turned away from churches because there is no compassion to help people, even when churches have the means to do so. I've heard excuses such as, "it's not our policy;" "that's not what the benevolence fund is for," "it's not our concern;" "it's not our issue;" "they got in the situation, they'll get themselves out;" "we can't help everybody;" I've literally heard every excuse in the book.

The compassion in my heart would never let me turn away someone hurting and in need. My wife and I share the same compassion and we've helped dozens of people in emergency situations, and probably ten times more than that who just were in need. Why? Because we've been in need, and also in crisis situations many times. That is why I believe I have such a passion for helping others.

Hospitals have support groups. Why not churches? If churches turn away the needy, where do they go? Wasn't the church established to help those in need? Wasn't that part of the mission of Jesus when He laid the ground work for His church? At the time of editing this book for release I've planted a church. *Gospel and Grace Christian Church* plans to open its doors soon. It will be one that has "helping people in need" as part of its mission, core values, and vision for helping to build up people into mature, responsible, caring Christians whose purpose is helping people, not holding on to the purse strings.

Members help churches; churches should help members.
It's a simple concept.

Writing about establishing ministries to help today's problems reminds me of a story from the Bible that is still plaguing our society today. Over the past several years, same sex couples have been fighting for the right to wed and be considered married in the same context as God's Biblical Covenant. While we know, and they know, that God's Covenant of marriage is between one man and one woman, during this recent public battle, which was voted on during an election, I could not help but remember the story of how God destroyed Sodom and Gomorrah for such similar lewdness.

While I watched in awe the clever TV ads, what I learned from watching this play out in the media, is that the people who were voting to approve marriage for same sex couples, were not voting against God's Covenant of marriage between one man and one woman, they were in fact, voting against God, His Will, His Way, and His Word.

They were saying yes to their own way of life, and no to the way God established for us to live this life.

They were saying yes to doing it their own way, and no to the rules and regulations God set in His word.

They were saying yes to making their own laws, and no to the commandments God created.

I can only pray that one day God opens their eyes to see His truth.

This may shock you, but ask yourself this question:

Can a person still be considered Christian if they are obeying all of God's other laws, except one? And that one is where they do not want God's input when it comes to their sexual preference? Before you answer, let me add that some will make the argument that the Bible says whoever is guilty of breaking one commandment is guilty of breaking them all (James 2:10). But marriage between one man and one woman is not a commandment, it's God's covenant.

Now, here's the part that may shock you:

How then, are any of us considered Christians given the fact that we've all sinned and fallen short of the glory of God.

Again, before you answer, here's how:

A sinner is considered forgiven once that person confesses their sin, repents, and doesn't do it anymore. This is how the vast majority of Christians live their lives and continue hoping for salvation.

But, those who live in sin, know they are living in sin, refuse to stop, and consider their sin 'a lifestyle' 'a sexual preference' 'the way they were born', the Bible is crystal clear:

"For if we sin wilfully after that we have received the knowledge of the truth, there remaineth no more sacrifice for sins. But a certain fearful looking for of judgment and fiery indignation, which shall devour the adversaries." Hebrews 10:26-27

We are commanded to show love to sinners, and hate their sin. So while a homosexual is still considered very much a Christian, how does the church respond to this volatile issue? Easily, with God's love. God loved you, and me, when we were in sin. Do the same for them.

We know that in the early days of humanity God allowed man to have more than one wife. In fact men were allowed hundreds of them, and a bunch of mistresses on the side. That's Old Testament, which means that it's Old Covenant. In the New Testament, under the New Covenant that Jesus ushered in, man should have *one* wife. And still 'thou shalt not commit adultery' applies. Besides, God would probably rather change His mind about letting men have multiple wives and mistresses on the side, than deal with the wrath of millions of angry women who oppose that. [Laugh - that's a joke].

Let me point out that Exodus 20:14 says 'thou shalt not commit adultery', which *is* a commandment, and also falls within the construct of God's Covenant of Marriage. In my opinion, there are many more people who commit adultery that those practicing the sins of sodomy and homosexuality, but we aren't having any voting battles on adultery yet. Sin is sin, period. And everyone who has ever heard the word of God preached into their hearing knows what sin is. And unrepented sin, will result in death come judgment day. So, again, while a homosexual is still considered a Christian, how does the church respond to this volatile issue? Easily, by dealing with 'sin' the same way Jesus did: With Love.

Churches need to create ministries to confront and address this and many other volatile issues so that people can be forgiven, delivered, healed, and set free from the sin they are living in. People have free will, and even if they pretend they don't, they know right from wrong.

Let's go to the Scripture 1st Timothy 4:1 where the Bible identifies 'Seducing spirits', and talk about this for a moment so you can understand what is it churches are dealing with in this volatile issue.

SEDUCING SPIRITS come in many forms and offer many things. But in order to understand them, and how they operate, we must first look to the Scripture that identifies them.

1. Proverbs 7

Described as a strange woman; a stranger that flattereth with her words; attired as a harlot; loud and stubborn; and...married. A spirit that went outside, seduced a man, and took him home with her.

2. Genesis 19

Described as the men of the city; even the men of Sodom. A spirit that asked Lot to let them have sex with the male Angels that were in his house, and refused to offer of Lot's daughters over the Angels.

3. Luke 4:2

Described as the devil, who tempted Jesus Himself for 40 days.

There were many other seducing spirits the Bible referenced, such as Mrs. Pottiford, and churches need to identify and expose them.

And remembering what happened to Sodom and Gomorrah one must also remember what happened BEFORE that village was destroyed, in that God also destroyed an entire planet of people for their wickedness, only leaving eight behind to start over.

So, God is not mocked. And He will bring His word to pass. So it truly does not matter who practices what sin, or how long they're living in it, or how rebellious they are while doing it, if they have not repented of it by the time God's appointed time to fulfill the prophecies of the book of Revelation, they are most likely going to hell.

So you see, not much has changed. People are still disobeying God. They are still wanting things their own way, rather than living by God's rules, regulations, laws, commandments and even authority.

The only difference is that in the past, God was vocal and lived with us, on the planet, and dealt with sin almost immediately and with a wide stroke of His hand.

Today, since He ascended back to Heaven after taking a beating, from us, to the point of tearing apart the flesh from His bone, He has been quietly dealing with sin through His word, His preachers, and His patience. Showing people what to do through His word. Telling people what to do through His preachers. And being patient for us to repent and return to Him, so He can return to us. If you think about it, it's truly an amazing concept and construct that we don't deserve.

When God, in the flesh, via the manifested form of Jesus the Christ, ascended back to Heaven, He left behind specific instructions for us to continue on with, carry on with, and be led by. And for many centuries, people have tried to do just that. Carry on.

However, let's bring that very statement to today. And let me help you to understand why things happen the way they do.

You know this next scenario, and at some point in your life, have probably participated in it. And, it's one that is constantly shown on television. What am I talking about? Simple: I'm talking about what happens to the students once the teacher leaves the classroom.

In almost EVERY classroom, the moment the teacher steps away from the class for even just a few minutes, without another adult, or person of leadership left behind in that classroom, the students think it's their duty to act up. To fall into chaos. To stop being the students that were just quiet and respectful of the teacher.

This is the very reason that it is VITAL for the pastors, priests, reverends, shepherds, and other church leaders to practice what we preach. It is imperative, mandatory, and necessary for us to lead the sheep that are sitting in our pews as the congregation, into learning how to DO THE WORD through ministry work. Sheep cannot lead sheep. So if the shepherd does not lead them, the natural instinct is for them to wander around aimlessly amongst themselves.

The problem is, while they are sitting in that pasture called a Bible study class, or Sunday school class, they are there, as sheep, to learn what it is they are supposed to do at this level, and the next.

But I've learned through many years of teaching, and observing, that if the shepherd does not lead the sheep into DOING THE WORK of the ministry, the sheep will never feel comfortable enough to step outside of the safety and sanctuary of the protective church walls, in order to be used by God away from the pasture.

So the sheep sit there, coming back again, week after week, never knowing that they are supposed to be taking the years of training they have already received and doing something with it other than coming to **Church On Sunday** and doing **Nothing On Monday.**

There are many ministries and opportunities for the shepherd to lead the sheep into. In fact, God outlined it in His word in Ephesians 2:10. The work has been prepared in advance for us to DO. Without this work, Christians (sheep) would have no one in need to feed, to clothe, to shelter, to house, to minister to when they're in prison, to visit when they are sick, to take care of when they get older, or to help while they are in orphanages.

Christians (sheep) have a clearly defined path, walked by JESUS first, that we are supposed to continue to follow, as HIS SHEEP, once we have received the training and are mature enough to do so.

Let's discuss some of the problems that exist in many churches and in every community, that church leaders should be using it's trained sheep, to help provide some form of support for, and working to address head on. You'll see, the first problem, is also the first solution.

EROSION OF THE FAMILY UNIT

Family is our first ministry. It is the foundation of God's Kingdom. It is how we keep connected to God. It is the basis of everything Godly. It is the basic structure of who we are as people. The family has been under attack since satan was abdicated from the family of God, and kicked out of Heaven for trying to elevate himself above God. Since then, satan has been trying to do everything he can to make the lives of others as miserable as his own by causing rifts between family members. Anytime he succeeds, families are torn apart.

Churches can respond to this head on by holding support groups and mediation sessions with families before, during, and after problems surface because it helps start the process of forgiveness and healing. And, it takes the power away from the devil.

There is nothing better that a church can do, than to show members of its congregation, and its community, that it cares about a family. Taking one person, and/or one family at a time, and helping to meet their needs to keep them from struggling not only strengthens the foundation under and support around that person and/or family, but it lets others know where to get support when they are in need.

CRIME

As someone who lived a life of crime for 2/3rds of my existence, people could say I should write a book on the subject, and they would be right. Because I have. It's titled, *The Psychology of Crime Is a Lesson For Life.* My reason for writing it was simple. I had to study myself, looking back from my childhood, in order to understand what could have motivated me to make such stupid decisions, mistakes, and wrong turns.

What I learned about myself, is something that churches can and should use as a primer to help its leaders, members, and community deal with crime head on. The number one thing I learned about myself was that I committed crimes out of rebellion, out of anger, out of opportunity, out of an outright refusal to respect authority, and a sometimes blatant disregard for the property and belongings of others. Knowing right from wrong didn't stop me, when I was intent upon hurting myself, and others. This is the one thing that churches can use to help people in their congregation and their community, who commit crime, face up to what they do and have done, in order to start the healing process. How? By exposing the crime, and the criminal. Why? Because it wasn't until the things I was doing were exposed, that I was able to look at them myself. My mind was clouded from years of wrongdoing that only stopped after cameras were constantly in my face, and victims kept showing up in court, making me face what I had done. At the time it was painful, but I'm grateful for it today. The Bible says expose sin. And we should follow God's word.

Exposing crime within your church does several things, including:

1. It takes the power away from the devil. What power? The power to use it against you 'successfully'; I didn't say he won't try, I said he won't be successful.

2. It keeps the devil from using the crime you're trying to keep secret, from being used by him to create lies, deception, and all sorts of other things that are built up around a crime, including the thought that if you got away with it once, you can attempt it again.

3. It keeps gossip from taking root and spreading out of control. I didn't say people won't gossip, because they probably will. But exposing the crime keeps the gossip at bay. Because there's normally not anything for gossipers to tell others about, if they already know.

4. Exposing one person's crime serves as a warning to others to not do something they may be thinking of, because it will be exposed.

5. It also helps serve as a powerful tool for deliverance because it lets those in your congregation and in the community know that you care enough about their deliverance to help them face and get through this stronghold in their lives, regardless of who knows it.

6. It keeps the person who committed the crime from having to stress about it, just to try and keep it a secret.

ABSENTEE DADS

People die. That's a fact of life. And when they do, they can no longer provide the parenting necessary to help children left behind grow and mature into adults. That is exactly why and when churches need to step in and provide the support needed to help that family cope, and get through the stress and strain of having to carry on without the head of household in that position any longer.

That's exactly what happened in my life. In 1980, my dad passed away. It was 8 years after my mom died. We were members of a methodist church at the time, but I never saw, or heard from any of the members after he passed. And my sister had even worked at the church as the pastor's secretary.

Churches need to step up and follow God's word at this point in any family that experiences the tragedy of death. Churches need to follow the parable of leaving the 99 lost sheep to find the one that was lost. Why? Because I believe it could have helped keep me from being lost, straying away, and out of contact with the church, for the next 17 years of my life. After my dad passed, I didn't return to the safety of God's arms for 17 years, 1994, when I was 34 years old. And although I do not blame that church for what happened in my life during those 17 years, I truly believe that it holds some level of responsibility for not ever reaching out to me or my family during our time of crisis and need. I pray that this personal testimony helps you see the need for churches to help a family when dads cannot.

SPOUSAL ABUSE

Many churches are afraid to come between, get involved, or cross the boundary between husband and wife. But when spousal abuse is taking place, and the spouse being abused has come to you for help, do not turn your back, close your door, or retreat into your church office as if you can't or shouldn't get involved. <u>God can help them, through you, IF you let Him use you to do it!</u> Married couples will argue, disagree, yell at each other, go for days not talking, and a whole host of other things when they are married. But when that arguing has escalated to laying hands on each other, or one of the other, it is the responsibility of the church to step in. And yes, it happens both ways. Men are abused by women spouses as well. But for the sake of this book, and this short description, I will use what society deems as the traditional 'man abusing his wife' scenario.

When the wife comes to the church for help in this situation, it is imperative for the church to step up and provide the protection, and direction needed to help the wife out of that situation. Often, in the news, we hear where these situations have turned so violent that the wife (and sometimes even the kids) ends up dead. My first thought, is normally, where was the church in this situation? Did the church play any part at all in trying to help the spouse being abused get the legal, social, or counsel they needed to get out of the situation before it resulted in death? Churches are supposed to **stand in the gap** for others. And according to James 2:14-16, that does not just mean simply praying for someone in need, but doing nothing else.

SPIRITUAL DECLINE

Spiritual decline has been happening since the beginning of human existence. It started in the Garden of Eden and progressively worsened over time. And within the past 40-50 years, decency, ethics, standards, and any hope of maintaining what was, has been replaced by all sorts of moral decay.

The people that are involved in and participate in such decline know that they are doing so. For example, it is no secret when you are making a TV show that there is a possibility that young kids may just happen to see you kiss another man in a TV commercial even if the parents of those kids are watching something totally not related to such activity. There is also the possibility, given the battles in the courts and during elections, that young kids may be taught that it is OK for two women to be married to each other, even though God says it is not.

Spiritual decline did not just start in this century. It has been around since Adam and Eve. The only difference is that now, more people are no longer afraid of publicly denouncing God, His morals, His values, His laws, or His commandments. Many feel it is more important to please one person for one moment in time, no matter how long that moment lasts, than it is to please the God who created them. Churches, need to continuously and consistently take a firm stand against spiritual decline, moral decay, and do so publicly. Because somebody has to stand up for what is right in God's eyes.

INCARCERATED PARENTS

I've been incarcerated more than once. Each time it was because I made bad decisions about business, which cost banks, and real hard-working people, tens to hundreds of thousands of dollars, that they could not, or did not recoup from investing in a business of mine.

Being incarcerated did not scare Jesus away. And it should not scare the church away. In fact, Jesus inserted 'ministering to prisoners' as one of the requirements for ministry needed to help prevent Christians from ending up in the line with others headed for hell.

Again neither time I was incarcerated did my church step up or embrace my family. They offered no support. If it wasn't for one man who made a sacrifice to help my wife and kids move out of our home in a gated community, they may not have had any support at all.

It is vitally important for churches to lead by example by using the act of forgiveness, and embrace someone who has made a mistake and ended up being incarcerated for it. Without this embrace, many members of the congregation will shun, blame, and withdraw themselves from the individual(s), and often end treating them as lepers.

Churches must show compassion to those who are and have been incarcerated and their family. The way to do this is to take the person, train and include them in the same positions and processes and rights and responsibilities that other members have the benefit of.

BROKEN RELATIONSHIPS

Members leave churches all the time. But in most of the churches I've been in, and even the two I've been members of over 15 years, I've yet to see one church that gets this right. In the parable of the lost sheep, Jesus explains that a shepherd has one hundred sheep, and one gets lost, the shepherd is supposed to leave the 99 in order to go find the one that was lost.

When churches neglect to do this vitally important task, members who left and lost their way, are most often waiting and hoping for the pastor, priest, bishop, reverend, preacher, or anyone in the church leadership to come and see about them. I've spoken with dozens of people who left both the churches I've been in over 15 years, and asked them one simple question: *"Did anyone come and see about you, check on you, or even call to ask you why you left and what they could do to help you find your way back?"* The answer was the same in all conversations. It was a resounding 'no'.

When relationships are broken between a church and an individual or even a family, God intends for the church to take the lead to help restore it; rebuild it; repair it.

The goal of any local church should and must be to help its members get ushered in to the Heavenly Church, which is the Kingdom of God. In order to do this, churches must not let sheep stay lost without at least making an effort to get them back in the flock.

MONEY MANAGEMENT

In my book *Credit Debt and Income For Christians* I discuss how vitally important it is for Christians to get out from under any and all financial debt. In Galatians 5:1 Jesus set the standard for us to be free from all such strongholds. Debt is bondage. Once it has you it keeps you working many years of your life just to keep paying the interest on the principal. Until you learn how to just pay off the principal and avoid interest, buy assets not liabilities, you will never escape. The book talks about and teaches many ways to eliminate debt. At my peak, I've been in more than a million dollars in debt to investors, taxes, and personal creditors, and have had to file bankruptcy several times. This is not at all a normal cycle or circumstance for any Christian, and it should be avoided like the plague.

In my book *Witness Protection Program For Christians* I teach how paying your Tithes can help protect you from the bondage of debt, if you're obedient to God's process. Anytime and literally every time you step outside of the process, meaning receiving income without paying Tithes on it, as a Christian, you fall into a cycle of unforeseen circumstances, which God calls curses, that lasts until you get back in line with God's will, God's way, and God's process of protection.

Churches need to hold regular classes to teach money management, fiscal responsibility, basic economics, debt elimination, budgeting, and a host of other topics that help its members stay away from, get free of, and get out from under the bondage and stronghold of debt.

JOBLESSNESS AND CAREER PURSUITS

In my book *Build Your Resume The Right Way* I focused on giving the reader a resume roadmap for success in the job market or career pursuit. Each of these is distinctly different.

A job comes with a certain level of requirements, which produces little except basic income in return and often carries with it, hesitance, stress, and dread about even going to work.

A career, however, incites the imagination, spurs growth and gain, pushes you into planning, encourages practices such as persistence and patience, and provides assurances such as benefits, bonuses, profit sharing and/or stock options, retirement incentives, management opportunities, severance packages, and much more.

~ A job can be started in a day, any day.
~ A career takes time to lay a foundation for, be educated about, get the training and professional development needed to chart the course.

~ Most jobs can turn into a career at just about any point, depending on the employer.
~ Most careers rarely revert back into a job.

Churches that can afford it should employ its members, and/or develop a course to teach its members how to reach their career goals especially in areas of ministry.

ADDICTION AND RECOVERY

God delivered me from drug addiction September 12, 1991. I smoked marijuana daily, and experimented with crack the entire summer of 1987 because I could afford it. I've never liked the taste or effects of alcohol, but until 1991 I drank lager beer occasionally.

Being delivered means just that. On that day, God removed the taste, desire, or want of any of these things from my life and I've never looked back since. Never wanted them since. Never thought about them since. To be a living witness to His power and ability is truly amazing. God is an awesome God who is worthy to be praised.

Churches need to meet addiction and recovery head on. Every church has someone addicted to some thing. It does not necessarily have to be drugs. It could be pornography. It could be alcohol. But whatever it is, churches need to provide support groups, counseling, prayer sessions, classes, and any and all training available to its leadership on how to handle, manage, confront, and cope with persons with such problems in their lives, because people, yes even church members, do have them, and yes, even seasoned saints can backslide.

Churches should teach it leadership how to spot, listen for, smell, and observe certain mannerisms associated with addicts and those in recovery. And, I would highly recommend churches select from members who have been through such addictions and been delivered from them, to be the leaders over these ministries and groups.

SPIRITUAL AND OTHER EDUCATION

At the time of the writing of this book, I've just been accepted in a Graduate school program to pursue my Doctorate in Church Leadership and Organization. This has been a dream of mine, a passion of mine, a pursuit of mine, a hope of mine, for many years. God willing, I plan to walk across the stage and receive this Degree upon completion of the required courses soon.

Churches should offer some form of Christian Education Classes that go 'beyond traditional Bible study', in order to help its members grow and mature in areas of church and ministry leadership that God has called them into, and gifted them for.

Churches that do not offer such classes should encourage members to locate and pursue such enhanced Christian Education so they can become better leaders, and prepare to walk into their own churches and ministries some day. I attended classes for many years during annual conventions and other training initiatives, and they helped me more than I could ever mention in this short book.

Churches should offer incentives such as scholarships for members to be awarded in circumstances where they cannot afford to attend classes on their own, or in situations where their academic merit has shown that they deserve such support. Churches can easily offer such programs and become accredited to do so, through a number of Christian Colleges and Universities that offer 'Affiliate' programs.

CHRONIC DISEASES

Sin and sickness were things that Jesus Christ carried to the cross with Him. He put both of these things to death so that we would not have to walk in them, or be tormented by them. And if we do the simplest of things, we have the assurance of Christ Himself, that we can avoid them.

Those simplest things include:
Eating the food God provides for us that grows from the Earth.
Not eating food created in labs with chemicals.

Drinking water and other beverages that God created and provides.
Not drinking beverages created in labs with chemicals.

Food and beverages that God created, that never runs out, gives us the natural nourishment and nutrition that we as God's children are supposed to have.

Food created in labs and with chemicals are designed to kill us. I've said it before, many people care more about the taste of a candy bar, than the effects of eating it. God never intended for us to eat anything that would cause us sickness and disease.

To get a much better understanding of how to create ministries that can help you help your members avoid chronic diseases by just changing diet, read my book, *Disease Carrier - Don't Be A Host For Sin.*

HEALTH AND WELLNESS

To be useful to God and effective in ministry, it is recommended that you start and/or maintain some form of physical exercise and healthy eating habits, ideally before or somewhere during, the time you surrender yourself as a willing vessel to do ministry work.

As a willing vessel, you are responsible for taking care of your health. While God is most certainly a Healer, and can remove all form of physical and spiritual disease from your body, God wants us to have the faith to make the effort that gives Him the incentive to do so.

Our health and wellness directly depends upon our willingness to walk in it. Once we're committed to walking in good health and wellness, we will train our bodies to treat chemical-based foods as poison, and want more and more God-given, natural foods.

Getting to, or maintaining good health and wellness is not an easy or overnight process, it takes work. But my argument that YOU CAN DO IT is based on this statement: *If you can get up each day and go to work for someone who probably cares nothing about whether you get to Heaven, you can work on yourself and work for God too.*

Churches need to help its members maintain good health and wellness by hosting classes around these topics. But some churches, are going to have to break the tradition and sin of gluttony that many have fallen into each week, and covering it with the title of Fellowship.

LACK OF MALE ROLE MODELS

At the release of this book, my wife and I have been together 28 years. We've raised two daughters (28 & 23); and are helping to raise two grandsons (6 & 4). My wife and I opened the doors in our home for strangers to live with us, 15 of our 28 years. And, we've been going to church as a family since 1997 and in leadership positions within two churches since 1997. None of this came easy.

I've been incarcerated multiple times, but we're still together.
I've had numerous failed businesses, but we're still together.
I've lost two fortunes in real estate, but we're still together.
I've made countless bad decisions, but we're still together.
I've used as well as sold drugs, but we're still together.
I've been a member of a gang, but we're still together.

Male role models exist in every church. And not that I would even quality for the distinction or title, society holds up athletes, actors, musicians, and entertainers as role models, and churches should do exactly the opposite.

JESUS the CHRIST should be our ultimate role model. And there are some instances where Earthly role models are and can be of great help to members who are looking for men who they can be mentored or trained up by. Churches, should hold support groups and create ministries that help foster growth and development of male role models and strong men of faith, members can count and depend on.

POVERTY AND LACK

Poverty is not something God ordained for born-again believers to suffer under. Those who have surrendered their lives to God, through a relationship with His Son, Jesus Christ are Blessed with the same inheritance set aside for Christ. But, in order to receive it, you have to be in God's will, and living within His purpose.

Being in lack does not necessarily mean you are broke without money. It could mean you lack the faith necessary to move the mountain of lack away from you, and the mountain of finance toward you. God's word clearly tells and teaches us that if we seek Him first, and His righteousness, all these things will be added unto us. It also says that God will Bless us according to His riches in glory. And, tells us that if we delight ourselves in Him, He will give us the desires of our heart.

Many churches need to teach classes regularly on how to help its members grow beyond poverty and lack. God's will is for us to have abundance, primarily so that we can be a Blessing to others. But also so we can show others that God is a God of His word and when we live by His word, He blesses us from His word.

The Bible also says to whom much is given much is required. We should be careful how and what we see as ways to get free of poverty and lack, because there are some very dangerous temptations lurking around such as the love of money, ready to grab hold of us and not let go. It held on to me for over 25 years of my life.

	CHAPTER FIVE
R **E** **C** **A** **P**	Ministering To Today's Problems • Erosion of the Family Unit • Crime • Absentee Dads • Spousal Abuse • Spiritual Decline • Incarcerated Parents • Broken Relationships • Money Management • Joblessness and Career Pursuits • Addiction and Recovery • Spiritual and Other Education • Chronic Diseases • Health and Wellness • Lack of Male Role Models • Poverty and Lack

Chapter Six

PLACES TO MINISTER

"Go make disciples of all nations, baptizing them in the Name of the Father, and of the Son and of the Holy Spirit."

Matthew 28:19

Places To Minister

This is a very brief list of places you can do ministry work. I suggest you develop your own list over time because at some point you'll need it to start sharing your transformation with others who need to do the same thing. The list of places to minister helps you follow what James 2:14-17 says. It's no good to see people in need and not do anything but pray for them. Faith without works is dead.

WHERE AND HOW TO FEED THE HUNGRY

- Start a food drive at your church and build a team.
- Make bag lunches (sandwiches, fruit, bottled water) to give away.
- Get 10 Delis to donate 10 sandwiches a month to feed 100 people.
- Volunteer at shelters in their food line.
- Create flyers to post at grocery stores on their public boards.
- Get permission from a grocery store to hold a bag at checkout.
- Check the Internet.
- Deliver postcards to everyone in your neighborhood.
- Put flyers on cars in your neighborhood/church parking lot.

People that are hungry hang out in parks, bus terminals, around homeless shelters, libraries, and many walk the streets downtown during the day. You can help. Develop a rapport with them from the moment you start bringing food. You can build a team of people. Each of your individual efforts can grow into a major food program if you follow the loaves and fishes model Jesus set as an example.

WHERE AND HOW TO CLOTHE THE NAKED

- I give away clothing I can't wear any longer.
- I ask others to give away clothing they can't wear any longer.
- I try and get one item per month from 50 people to give away.

- Call or visit department stores for stuff they throw away.
- Ask consignment shops for things they couldn't sell.
- Buy from thrift stores and give clothes away.

- Start a clothing drive at your church for winter (build a team).
- Many department stores have foundations you can apply at.
- Visit garage sales and ask people to give you stuff they didn't sell.

- Place flyers on every car in your neighborhood.
- Deliver postcards to everyone in your neighborhood.
- Check the Internet.

- Ask landlords to give you stuff renters leave behind.
- Ask moving companies to give you stuff movers never picked up.
- Ask storage places to donate stuff from lockers they auction.

I know it's hard to believe but not everyone has clothes. Especially when people are coming out of prison with no family support once they are released. But they are expected to immediately go on job interviews and land a job with the same clothes they wore in prison. A team of people with a focused effort, can make a major impact.

<u>WHERE AND HOW TO VISIT THE SICK</u>

- Volunteer at nursing homes.

- Volunteer at hospices.

- Volunteer at senior homes.

- Volunteer at hospitals in ICU.

- Volunteer at hospitals in burn units.

- Volunteer at hospitals in cancer wards.

- Volunteer at veteran's homes.

- Check the Internet.

- Build a team at your church.

Again, in the mid 80s I was the Personal Care Attendant for a retired dentist name Fred Phoenix. He was bedridden from a stroke. His wife, Hazel, also a retired dentist, had no help.

I was able to use the compassion God had placed in me when caring for my dad when he was sick in late 70s, to help someone else.

The most important component of visiting the sick, is just to be in their presence. Some of them don't have family, and the only people they ever see are the people that work in the place they are at.

You and your team of people can have a major impact on the lives of the sick in many ways.

WHERE & HOW TO HELP STRANGERS FIND HOMES

- Place flyers at halfway houses.
- Call landlords in the newspapers.
- Establish a relationship with prisons for release-day-info.

- Check the Internet.
- Check your city's chamber of commerce.
- Call your local Salvation Army or Gospel Mission.

- Build a team at your church for other resources.
- Hit the streets. Homeless are nearly everywhere.
- Hand out flyers outside libraries and bus stations.

Homeless people are everywhere. They hang out outside libraries, bus stations, and often walk the streets downtown. My focus is to help those coming out of prison, but yours doesn't have to be. There are homeless people on the streets who are not coming out of prison.

I help people coming out of prison because it is a ministry that's close to my heart, because of my experiences. There is no shortage of people coming out of prison. And, once you've helped one person connect with a good landlord and find housing; the Blessing will certainly be spread to others who need help. Sending letters to chaplains in prisons and jails to let them know you are available to help, can also make a huge impact. Prepare yourself for work, because finding housing is ministry work that helps strangers in any economy.

WHERE AND HOW TO MINISTER TO PRISONERS

•   Send letters, newsletters and other material by mail.

Receiving mail and getting visitors in prison is like gold. It lets people know that someone cares and that you're not alone.

•   Drop off books, booklets, tracts, and Bibles to prison chaplains.

Reading material in prison is a commodity. Sitting in a cell 20 hours a day gives you time to read and not much else.

•   Deliver books, booklets, tracts, and Bibles to halfway houses.

Once someone gets out of prison, having the right material to provide info on housing, churches, jobs, and other things are helpful.

•   Help ex-prisoners locate housing and jobs.

Without stable housing upon release from prison, everything else an ex-offender tries to accomplish, fails.

•   Hold Bible class inside the prison, workhouse, jail, halfway house.

Volunteers are always needed to represent Jesus inside the jail.

•   Volunteer at the Juvenile Detention Center.

More and more youth these days are getting into trouble. Because of the wide variety of temptations satan and people lost in the world dangles in front of them, help is always needed in this area.

•   Build a team at your church.

WHERE & HOW WOMEN CAN CARE FOR WIDOWS

- Take them to the grocery store or go for them.
- Get some men to volunteer to help with lawn care/snow removal.
- Chauffeur to doctor's appointments/pick up meds/hair cuts.
- Play board games and card games with them.
- Take them out for walks in their neighborhood.
- Help them create scrapbooks and photo albums.
- Help them clean, sort, and remove clutter.
- Take them to bingo and social events.
- Build a team at your church.

WHERE & HOW MEN CAN CARE FOR WIDOWERS

- Take them to the grocery store or go for them.
- Get some men to volunteer to help with lawn care/snow removal.
- Chauffeur to doctor's appointments/pick up meds/hair cuts.
- Play board games and card games with them.
- Take them out for walks in their neighborhood.
- Help them create scrapbooks and photo albums.
- Help them clean, sort, and remove clutter.
- Take them fishing and to bingo.
- Build a team at your church.

This is a small list, but every widow and widower needs help, especially if they have no family or have no family around to help with these things. Your presence can make a huge impact. And, the fact that they did it for us, makes them deserving of any help we give.

WHERE AND HOW TO SPEND TIME WITH ORPHANS

- Volunteer at orphanages to read books.
- Volunteer with Big Brother/ Big Sisters.
- Volunteer at Boys or Girls Clubs.
- Check the Internet.
- Build a team at your church.

My wife and I have raised two children, both daughters, ages 28 and 23 at the time of this writing. Now, we're taking the lead in raising our two grandsons, ages 6 and 4, because for a while, their dad wasn't around. So, children are near and dear to our heart.

Orphans need people in their lives just like kids who have both, or even just a single parent at home.

I suggest volunteering at a local orphanage. But if you want to do something global, there are many organizations where you can sponsor a child from another country; or go to food export centers where you can volunteer time to help prepare food, clothing and medicine packs, that will be delivered to orphanages in other countries.

Whatever your choice and focus, do something. Every little bit helps and every time I look at my own children and grandchildren, it motivates me to stay active, get involved, and make a conscious effort to help make the world better for other children who aren't as blessed as my own.

Why Not Just Church?

Now that you've read why and how to do ministry work outside the church walls, there are some final things you should know.

1. Faith without works is dead. So is church without ministry.

2. Many churches have walked away from missions and ministry, to embrace membership and money. The result is a big building, full of people of faith, but no works.

3. In Revelations chapter 2, Jesus sent letters to the seven churches, To five of the churches Jesus told them, "I know your works". Again, church worship and ministry work go hand in hand.

4. In Hebrews chapter 10 the writer gives a call to persevere. In verses 24-25 it says "let us consider how we may encourage one another on toward love and good works". Verse 25 says "Let us not give up meeting together (having church) as some are in the habit of doing." Whatever you do in ministry, don't stop having church. You must do both. There are numerous reference in the Gospel where Jesus had church, then did ministry work the rest of the time. He went around feeding the hungry, visiting and healing the sick, ministering and freeing prisoners, helping strangers, caring for widows, and spending time with orphans.

5. God bless you in church worship and in ministry work.

In Jesus Name, Amen.

Gentle Reminders

YOU, A FRIEND, AND THEIR FRIEND
= 3 SOURCES FOR FOOD

THERE ARE MANY PLACES
TO ASK FOR AND GET CLOTHING

THE BEST WAY TO VISIT THE SICK
IS TO JUST BE THERE

PEOPLE HAVE OTHER THINGS TO DO
THAN SPEND TIME WORRYING ABOUT HOUSING

HELP YOUTH IN TROUBLE
NOT BECOME ADULT PRISONERS

YOUR HELP CAN MAKE AN IMPACT
IN WIDOW'S & WIDOWER'S GOLDEN YEARS

ORPHANS JUST WANT TO BE LOVE
JUST LIKE EVERYONE ELSE

Contact

Author: Keith Hammond
President
Lessons For Life Books, Inc.
7455 France Avenue South #305
Edina, MN 55435

(952) 884-5498 ofc
(952) 884-3785 fax

author@LessonsForLifeBooks.com

web: LessonsForLifeBooks.com
mobile: m.LessonsForLifeBooks.com

How to Find Us:
Google:
'keith hammond lessons for life books'

Barnes & Noble:
bn.com
'keith hammond'

Bookwire.com
'keith hammond'

Amazon:
'keith hammond' plus 'book title'

Kindle:
'keith hammond' plus 'book title'

Catalog Reminder:
The best way to get an overall view of the more than 80 books I've written, is to download the full-color, interactive catalog from our website.

LessonsForLifeBooks.com/catalog.html

Every book page has a link to the preview of that book, and includes ISBN info, ordering info, etc.

Keep Up With Us!

Get our Mobile App at
m.LessonsForLifeBooks.com

Check our News section
on our website
for a calendar of
upcoming events
such as
Meet The Author

We are constantly
giving talks and hosting
casual readings
at local libraries
and coffee shops.

Hope to see you there soon!

See Our Categories!

The 81 books
written by
Author, Keith Hammond,
are detailed in one
convenient brochure.

Download it today at
LessonsForLifeBooks.com
/brochure.pdf

CATEGORIES

How To Study Your Bible
Building Your Church and Ministry
Discipleship Teaching and Training
Evangelizing in the End Time
Supercharging Your Faith and Works
The Holy Spirit
Info for New Believers and New Members
Sin and Salvation
Spiritual Growth
Testimony and Overcoming
Tithing, Stewardship and Giving
Worship, Prayer, Obedience and Sacrifice

REMEMBER
JESUS SENT OUT MINISTRY LEADERS
IN TWOS AND TEAMS.

Follow His lead, and leaders will follow yours.

Keith Hammond

Lessons For Life Books

PUBLISHERS

L E S S O N S F O R L I F E B O O K S . C O M